READY FOR TAKEOFF!
ENGLISH FOR STUDY ABROAD

Alan Jackson   Hiroko Uchida

KINSEIDO

Kinseido Publishing Co., Ltd.

3-21 Kanda Jimbo-cho, Chiyoda-ku,
Tokyo 101-0051, Japan

Copyright © 2020 by   Alan Jackson
                                   Hiroko Uchida

First published 2020 by Kinseido Publishing Co., Ltd.

Cover design   Takayuki Minegishi
Text design   C-leps Co., Ltd.
Illustrations   Atsuko Minato

Photos

p. 54 © Julien Viry | Dreamstime.com
p. 81 © Psstockfoto | Dreamstime.com (left)

🎧 音声ファイル無料ダウンロード

http://www.kinsei-do.co.jp/download/4105

この教科書で 🎧 DL 00 の表示がある箇所の音声は、上記 URL または QR コードにて
無料でダウンロードできます。自習用音声としてご活用ください。

▶ PC からのダウンロードをお勧めします。スマートフォンなどでダウンロードされる場合は、
　ダウンロード前に「解凍アプリ」をインストールしてください。
▶ URL は、検索ボックスではなくアドレスバー (URL 表示欄) に入力してください。
▶ お使いのネットワーク環境によっては、ダウンロードできない場合があります。

◉ CD 00　左記の表示がある箇所の音声は、教室用 CD（Class Audio CD）に収録されています。

はしがき

本書は、短期留学・語学研修で必要になる基本的な英語力を身につけることを目標とした
テキストです。出発前から帰国までの場面別に、多様なタスクを通じて重要表現の定着や
総合的な英語力の育成を目指します。外国語でのコミュニケーションにおいて大切なこと
は「シンプルな表現で」「正しく伝える」ことです。本書で学ぶことにより、皆さんが自分
の英語にさらに自信をつけてくれることを願っています。

本書の構成は以下の通りです。

Warm-up

実際の留学の場面で目にする様々な文書に目を通し、まずは情報をざっと読み取ります。

Listening 1: Short Talk

A Warm-up に関連した短いトークを聞いて、簡単な問題に答えます。

B トークの詳細を理解するため、音声をもう一度聞いてスクリプトの穴埋めに取り組みます。
完成したスクリプトを使って音読練習を行ってもよいでしょう。

Check with Your Partner! スクリプトの内容について、ペアで質問に答えます。

Key Phrases

各ユニットの重要表現です。音声と一緒に声に出して練習しましょう。

Practice

重要表現の練習問題です。[　] 内の語句をヒントに英文を完成させましょう。

Listening 2: Conversation

A 時間割や地図など、各ユニットの場面に沿った文書を読み、問題に答えます。

B A に関連した短い会話を聞いて、T/F 問題に答えます。

Your Turn to Talk

A B の準備段階として、Listening 2: Conversation と同様の文書が提示されます。

B A の内容を踏まえ、ペアワークでスピーキング活動を行います。

Key Phrases Review

各ユニットで学んだ重要表現（Key Phrases）をおさらいします。

Word Power!

各ユニットの重要語句が日本語訳付きでリストされています。空所には新しく学んだ語句を書
き加えましょう。

Preface

Study abroad is a great chance to connect with a different world, to test yourself and grow, and to acquire valuable English skills through active learning.

However, you can only take advantage of the valuable opportunities afforded by study abroad — in class, in homestay, and in the community — if you actively seek out chances to use your English and participate enthusiastically in communication. To do this, you will need to go abroad well prepared, and it is the aim of this book to provide you with the thorough English language preparation you will need.

The key objectives of the book are:

a) To have students develop confidence and fluency in using English at a relatively simple level with all four skills

b) To provide students with specific knowledge of the language used in English-speaking societies in study-abroad situations such as travel, college, and homestay

These objectives are achieved by means of:

i) Exercises in each unit that proceed from reception to production, from language focus to communication, and from language control to freer expression

ii) The use of carefully selected material from actual study abroad situations

iii) Control of grammatical expressions to practice and review a wide range of important basic language structures

iv) Frequent repetition of key phrases and built-in review to make learning thorough

v) Careful selection of vocabulary with a glossary in each unit

vi) Varied and interesting activities that help maintain the interest level of students

How to Use this Book

Warm-up

Understand information provided in visuals such as charts, notices or schedules, etc.

Listening 1: Short Talk

A Listen to a short talk connected to the Warm-up and complete a simple exercise to check basic understanding.

B For a more detailed understanding, listen carefully to the talk again and fill the blanks with missing words. The completed script can then be used for reading aloud to practice pronunciation and intonation.

Check with Your Partner! Listening 1 concludes with a more productive Q&A exercise.

Key Phrases

To focus on important language items, practice repeating and reading these key phrases.

Practice

Make complete sentences using the key phrases with the hints in brackets.

Listening 2: Conversation

A The main unit topic introduced in the Warm-up is further developed here by providing additional information in a visual with a comprehension exercise.

B Listen to a study-abroad conversation that is related to the visuals in A, and check your understanding with true/false questions.

Your Turn to Talk

A The visual here is closely related to the one on the previous page, but instead of focusing on reading, the related exercise generally focuses on writing.

B To complete the 4-skill set, practice speaking with your partner.

Key Phrases Review

As a wrap-up, look back at the Key Phrases on the third page of the unit, and check what you have learned by completing these sentences.

Word Power!

The last page of each unit lists the important new vocabulary with Japanese translations. You can add other words to the list if you wish.

Ready for Takeoff!
— English for Study Abroad

Contents

Introducing Yourself

Unit Goals

● Talk about your university and major 　　大学と専攻について話す
● Talk about your club 　　　　　　　　　クラブ活動について話す
● Talk about your free-time activities 　　余暇活動について話す

Warm-up

Read this information about three Japanese college students and fill in blanks (1)-(3) with words from the box below.

3人の日本人大学生についての情報を読んで、空所（1）～（3）に入る語句を下から選んで書き入れましょう。

Name	Akito	Sora	Miu
University	Saga Gakuin U.	(2)	Rakuhoku U.
Major	☐ Chemistry ☐ Economics ☐ Engineering	☐ Social Welfare ☐ English ☐ Politics	☐ Philosophy ☐ Drama ☐ Biology
Club	None	Lacrosse	(3)
Likes	(1)	Playing sports	Writing

English Newspaper Club　　　Watching J.League soccer　　　Yonezawa U.

Listening 1: Short Talk

A *Listen to three Japanese students introducing themselves and check (☑) their majors in the chart above.*

3人の自己紹介を聞いて、上の表のそれぞれの専攻にチェック（☑）をしましょう。

 DL 02 ~ 04　 CD 02 ~ CD 04

B *Look at the script and listen again. Fill in the blanks.*

スクリプトを見ながら音声をもう一度聞いて、空所を埋めましょう。

🎧 DL 02 ~ 04   ◎ CD 02 ~ ◎ CD 04

Good morning. My name is Akito, and I'm majoring in economics at Saga Gakuin University. At the **1.**_____, I don't belong to a university club, but I really like watching J.League soccer. I often go to watch games on weekends.

Hi! My name is Sora, and I'm from **2.**_____. I'd like to be a social worker in the future, so I'm majoring in social welfare at Yonezawa University. I'm a member of the Lacrosse Club, so I'm always **3.**_____. I love playing sports!

Hello, everybody! I'm Miu, and I'm a 3rd-year biology student at Rakuhoku University. I **4.**_____ like English, so I'm a member of the English Newspaper Club. I would like to study abroad one day, maybe in England or Ireland.

Check with Your Partner!

With a partner, ask and answer these questions about the script.

上のスクリプトについて、ペアになって1~3の質問をお互いにしてみましょう。

1. What does Akito like doing?
2. What is Sora majoring in?
3. Does Miu belong to a club at her university?

DL 05 ~ 07  CD 05 ~ CD 07

Key Phrases

I'm majoring in ... at ...

🔊 What are you majoring in?
- I'm majoring in law at Tochigi University.

I belong to ... / I'm a member of ...

🔊 Which club do you belong to at college?
- I belong to the Drama Club.
- I'm a member of the Rugby Club.

I like / love / enjoy ...ing

🔊 What do you like doing in your free time?
- I really like meeting my friends.
- I enjoy playing basketball.

Practice

Answer these questions using the words in the brackets.

[　　] 内の語句を使って、質問に答えましょう。

1. What are you majoring in?　[I'm — international relations — Kagoshima City University.]

_____

2. Are you a member of a club?　[Yes, — belong — the Manga — .]

_____

3. What do you like doing in your free time?　[I — computer games and — J-Pop.]

_____

11

Listening 2: Conversation

A *Read the memo that Mika made before she wrote an email to her host family. Match the questions below with answers* a *-* e *.*

ミカがホームステイ先にメールを書く前に作ったメモを読みましょう。その後、下の1〜5の質問に対する返答として正しいものを、 a 〜 e から選びましょう。

● **About my study abroad plans**

a I'm going to go to Vancouver, Canada.

b I'm going to study at Simon Fraser University.

c I'm going to leave Japan on August 1st.

d I'm going to stay for three weeks.

e I'd like to visit Stanley Park while I'm in Vancouver.

● **About myself**

• I'm majoring in ...

• I belong to ...

• I really like ...

---

1. When are you going abroad?   (   )

2. Where are you going?   (   )

3. How long are you going for?   (   )

4. What would you like to do during your stay?   (   )

5. Where are you going to study?   (   )

B *Listen to Mika's conversation with her teacher about the memo, and circle T (true) or F (false) for the following sentences.*

ミカと先生がメモについて話すのを聞いて、次の文が正しければ T、誤っていれば F を丸で囲みましょう。

⬇ DL 08   ⊙ CD 08

1. Mika is majoring in nutrition.   **T   F**

2. She belongs to the Badminton Club.   **T   F**

3. She really likes going shopping with her friends.   **T   F**

Your Turn to Talk

A *Mika is writing an email to her host mother. Choose the correct words from the box below to complete her email.*

ミカは、ホストマザーに自己紹介メールを書いています。 1〜5の空所に入る語句を下から選んで書き入れ、メールを完成させましょう。

Dear Mrs. Hickey,

My name is Mika Taniguchi and I'm going to stay with you from August 1st for three weeks while I'm studying at Simon Fraser University.

I am a **¹**[   ]-year student at Matsuyama Women's University, and I am majoring in **²**[   ]. I have a part-time job at **³**[   ] and I also belong to **⁴**[   ]. As for my hobbies, I really like **⁵**[   ].

While I'm in Vancouver, I'd like to visit Stanley Park. I look forward to meeting you in August very much!

Best regards,
Mika

going shopping   nutrition   a street dance circle   2nd   an Italian restaurant

B *Now talk about yourself with your partner by changing the underlined parts in Mika's email and filling in the blanks.*

ミカが書いたメールの下線部と空所に自分の情報を入れて、自己紹介メールを書きましょう。その後、ペアになって発表しましょう。

Make sentences using the Key Phrases you learned in this unit.
このユニットで学んだ Key Phrases を使って文を作りましょう。

1. My friend _____ is majoring in _____ at _____.
2. He/She belongs to _____.
3. He/She really likes _____.

Word Power!

Study this list of important new words and phrases in this unit. You can complete the list by adding more words that you learned.

Unit 1 で登場した重要語句のリストです。空所には、その他に新しく学んだ語句を自由に書き入れ、オリジナルのリストを作りましょう！

English	Japanese
☐ major (n)	専攻
☐ social welfare	社会福祉
☐ politics	政治学
☐ philosophy	哲学
☐ major in (v)	～を専攻する
☐ belong to	～に所属する
☐ social worker	ソーシャルワーカー
☐ international relations	国際関係論
☐ nutrition	栄養学
☐ As for	～について言えば
☐ look forward to ...ing	～することを楽しみに待つ
☐ Best regards	（手紙の末尾で）敬具
☐	
☐	
☐	
☐	
☐	
☐	
☐	
☐	
☐	
☐	

A Geography Lesson

Unit Goals

- Talk about geographical location   地理的な場所について話す
- Talk about climate   気候について話す
- Explain your travel schedule   旅行の日程を説明する

Warm-up

Read the sentences below and choose the locations (a-d) on the map.

下の英文を読んで、各都市の場所を地図上のa～dから選びましょう。

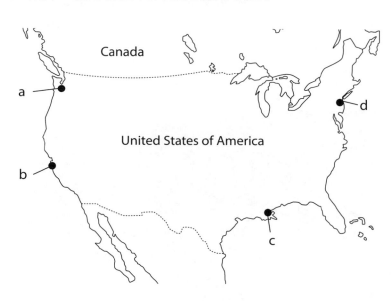

- **New Orleans** is in the southeast of the United States.   (   )
- **Seattle** is in the northwest of the United States.   (   )
- **New York** is on the east coast.   (   )
- **San Francisco** is on the west coast.   (   )

Listening 1: Short Talk

A *Listen to the teacher's talk about a trip to the U.S. Mark the route from Narita on the map.*

旅程についての先生の話を聞いて、地図上の都市を「成田（Narita）→経由地→目的地」の順に矢印で結びましょう。

B *Look at the script and listen again. Fill in the blanks.*

スクリプトを見ながら音声をもう一度聞いて、空所を埋めましょう。

🎧 DL 09　◎ CD 09

OK, everybody! Please listen. I'm going to **1.** _____ your trip to the U.S.

You are going to leave Narita Airport at 8:30 in the morning and fly to New Orleans **2.** _____ San Francisco on the west coast. You will finally arrive in New Orleans at 11:30 a.m. local time. Altogether, your trip will probably take about 17 hours. Your host family will meet you at the airport and take you to your homestay by **3.** _____. You'll probably get to your homestay at about 2:00 in the afternoon.

As for the weather, well, it's warmer in New Orleans than in Tokyo, so you won't need a winter coat. In February, it's about 15℃. On the other hand, it often rains, so you should always carry a **4.** _____ umbrella.

Check with Your Partner!

With a partner, ask and answer these questions about the script.

上のスクリプトについて、ペアになって1〜3の質問をお互いにしてみましょう。

1. Are the students going to fly directly to New Orleans?
2. What time will they arrive in New Orleans?
3. What does the teacher say about the temperature in New Orleans?

Key Phrases

It's in the [east/west] of … / It's on the [north/south] coast.

Seattle is in the northwest of the United States. It's on the west coast.
Sendai is in the northeast of Japan. It's on the east coast.

It's … ℃ (= degrees Celsius). / It often rains.

In Tokyo, it's about 5℃ in February, but it doesn't rain very much.
10℃ is 50°F (= degrees Fahrenheit).
It rains a lot, but it never snows in November.

I'm going to … / You will … / It will …

I'm going to tell you about your flight. You're going to leave at 9:00 a.m.
I think you'll arrive in San Francisco at 1:30 a.m. local time.
It'll probably take about an hour to get to your homestay in Baton Rouge, so you'll arrive at about 2:30.

Practice

Answer these questions using the words in the brackets.

[   ] 内の語句を使って、質問に答えましょう。

1. Where is Los Angeles?   [It's — the southwest — the United States.]

_____

2. Is it going to be cold tomorrow?   [No, it's — quite warm.] [about 20℃.]

_____

3. Do you think it'll rain?   [No, — never — April.]

_____

Listening 2: Conversation

A *Look at this map and answer the questions below.*

地図を見て、下の質問に答えましょう。

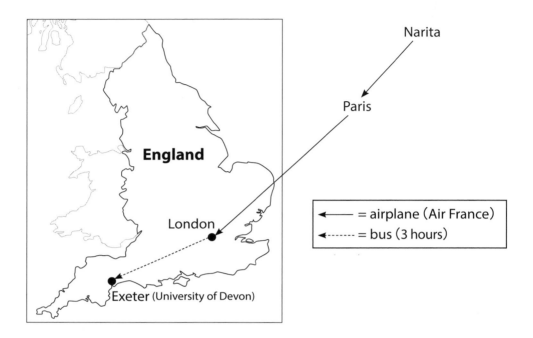

1. How are you going to get to England from Narita?

We're going to fly to _____ via _____ with _____ .

2. Where are you going to study?

We're going to study at the _____ in _____ .

3. Where's that?

It's on the south _____ of England. It takes about _____

to get there from London.

B *Listen to Hiroshi telling his Canadian friend Patrick about his trip to the UK, and circle T (true) or F (false) for the following sentences.*

ヒロシがカナダ人の友達パトリックに自分の英国旅行について話しているのを聞いて、次の文が正しければ T、誤っていれば F を丸で囲みましょう。

🎧 DL 13   💿 CD 13

1. It will take about 40 hours to get from Narita to London.　　T　F

2. A university teacher is going to pick Hiroshi up at Exeter Airport.　　T　F

3. It will probably be very cold when he arrives in Exeter.　　T　F

18

Your Turn to Talk

A *Use the key words to complete the sentences about a trip to Australia.*

キーワードを使い、オーストラリア旅行についての文を完成させましょう。

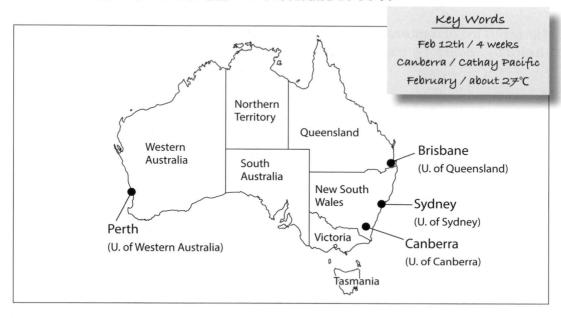

Key Words

Feb 12th / 4 weeks
Canberra / Cathay Pacific
February / about 27℃

I'm going to go to Australia on **1.**_____.

I'm going to spend **2.**_____ at the University of Canberra.

I'm going to fly to **3.**_____ via Hong Kong with

4._____.

In **5.**_____, the temperature is **6.**_____ in the daytime.

B *Pick one city from the map and plan your own trip. Talk about your plans with your classmate.*

上の地図から都市を一つ選んで、オリジナルの旅行プランを作りましょう。その後、クラスメイトとお互いが作ったプランについて話しましょう。

Review

Key Phrases

Make sentences using the Key Phrases you learned in this unit.

このユニットで学んだ Key Phrases を使って文を作りましょう。

1. I'm going to visit _____ next _____. It'll take

_____ to get there from my hometown.

2. My hometown is _____.

3. It _____ rains in my hometown in _____.

Unit 02
Word Power!

Study this list of important new words and phrases in this unit. You can complete the list by adding more words that you learned.

Unit 2 で登場した重要語句のリストです。空所には、その他に新しく学んだ語句を自由に書き入れ、オリジナルのリストを作りましょう！

English	Japanese
☐ geography	地理
☐ geographical location	地理的な場所
☐ climate	気候
☐ schedule	日程、スケジュール
☐ via	～経由で
☐ local time	現地時間
☐ altogether	全部で
☐ folding umbrella	折り畳み傘
☐ directly	直行で
☐ temperature	気温、温度
☐ Fahrenheit (°F) / Celsius (°C)	華氏／摂氏
☐ pick (s/o) up	～を迎えに行く、～を車に乗せて行く
☐ probably	恐らく
☐	
☐	
☐	
☐	
☐	
☐	
☐	
☐	
☐	
☐	
☐	

Unit 03

Arriving

Unit Goals

- Talk about travel experiences   旅行経験について話す
- Fill out arrival cards   入国カードに記入する
- Understand instructions and advice   指示と助言を理解する

Warm-up

Read this notice about immigration documents and answer the questions below.

入国審査で示す書類に関する注意書きを読んで、下の質問に答えましょう。

Immigration – Documents

You must have: - your passport
                   - your arrival card

You may need: - your letter of enrollment
                   - a bank statement
                   - your host family's address

Which document shows:

1. that you have enough money?   _____
2. the name of your course?   _____
3. information about your flight?   _____

Listening 1: Short Talk

A *Listen to the teacher's explanation about your arrival at Perth Airport in Australia. What does she say about food? Choose the best answer.*

オーストラリアのパース空港到着時についての先生の説明を聞きましょう。先生は食べ物について何と言っていますか。最もふさわしい答えを選びましょう。

 DL 14   CD 14

a. You may carry food into Australia, but only in your carry-on luggage.

b. You mustn't carry Japanese food into Australia.

c. You mustn't carry any fresh fruit or vegetables into Australia.

B *Look at the script and listen again. Fill in the blanks.*

スクリプトを見ながら音声をもう一度聞いて、空所を埋めましょう。

🎧 DL 14 💿 CD14

Have you ever flown abroad before? No? Nobody? Well, when you arrive at Perth Airport, you have to do the following:

First, go to immigration and hand your passport and arrival card to the immigration officer. The officer will probably ask you some questions, so please answer them **1.**_____. They may ask you for your letter of enrollment, a bank statement, or the address of your homestay, so you should **2.**_____ them in your carry-on luggage.

After immigration, you must pick up your suitcase in the baggage claim area and go to customs. The most **3.**_____ thing is this: Don't carry any fresh fruit or vegetables into Australia. They are very **4.**_____ about this.

Once you're finished with customs, you can go into the arrivals area to meet your host family.

Check with Your Partner!

With a partner, ask and answer these questions about the script.

上のスクリプトについて、ペアになって1～3の質問をお互いにしてみましょう。

1. Have the students ever flown abroad before?
2. What letter should they keep in their carry-on luggage?
3. Where must they pick up their suitcases?

 DL 15 ~ 17   CD 15 ~ CD 17

Key Phrases

Have you (ever) ... ?

🔊 Have you ever been to Australia?
- Yes, I have. I've been there twice.
- No, I've never been to Australia, but I've been to New Zealand.

What's your [name / date of birth / nationality] ?

🔊 What's your first name? - It's Simon.
What's your flight number? - It's AC1952.
What's your job? (What do you do?) - I'm a dentist.

You should ... / You must ... / Try to ...

🔊 You should answer questions politely.
You shouldn't tell any lies at immigration.
You must be honest.
You mustn't hide food in your suitcase.
Try to exercise on the plane. It prevents economy class syndrome.

Practice

Answer these questions using the words in the brackets.

[   ] 内の語句を使って、質問に答えましょう。

1. Have you ever been to Europe?   [Yes, — .] [France — Germany.]

_____

2. Should I buy insurance?   [Yes, you must — health — before you — Japan.]

_____

3. What's your advice about flying?   [Try — sleep — the plane.] [shouldn't — alcohol.]

_____

Listening 2: Conversation

A *Look at this New Zealand arrival card written by Masaki and answer the questions below.*

マサキの書いたニュージーランドの入国カードを見て、下の質問に答えましょう。

New Zealand Passenger Arrival Card

Flight number: NZ90   Aircraft seat number: 23A

Overseas port where you boarded this aircraft: Tokyo (Narita)

Passport number: TR4637881   Nationality as shown on passport: Japanese

Family name: Takahashi   Given or first name(s): Masaki

Date of birth: April 10th, 2002   Country of birth: Japan

Occupation or job: Student

Full contact address in New Zealand: 324 Eden Road, Auckland

---

1. What's Masaki's date of birth?   It's _____.

2. What's his nationality?   He's _____.

3. What's his passport number?   It's _____.

4. What airline did he fly with?

He _____ Air New Zealand.

5. Where is he going to stay while he is in New Zealand?

He's going to stay at _____.

B *Listen to the conversation between Masaki and an immigration officer at Auckland Airport, and circle T (true) or F (false) for the following sentences.*

オークランド空港でのマサキと入国管理官の会話を聞いて、次の文が正しければ T、誤っていれば F を丸で囲みましょう。

🎧 DL 18   ◎ CD 18

1. He has never been to New Zealand before.   T   F

2. In Auckland, he's going to stay with a family.   T   F

3. He's lost his arrival card.   T   F

Your Turn to Talk

A *Look at this New Zealand arrival card and fill in the blanks with your information.*

これはニュージーランドの入国カードです。空所にあなた自身の情報を書き入れましょう。

New Zealand Passenger Arrival Card

Flight number: NZ90   Aircraft seat number: 23A

Overseas port where you boarded this aircraft: Tokyo (Narita)

Passport number: _____   Nationality as shown on passport: _____

Family name: _____   Given or first name(s): _____

Date of birth: _____   Country of birth: _____

Occupation or job: _____

Full contact address in New Zealand: 324 Eden Road, Auckland

B *Now work with a partner. Ask and answer these questions about yourselves.*

ペアワークで旅行者と入国管理官になり、入国カードの内容について次の質問をしましょう。

· What's your passport number?   · What's your nationality?

· What's your family name?   · What's your given name?

· What's your date of birth?   · Where were you born?

· What's your occupation?   · Where are you going to stay?

Review

Key Phrases

Make sentences using the Key Phrases you learned in this unit.

このユニットで学んだ Key Phrases を使って文を作りましょう。

1. I've been to _____, but I've never been to _____.

2. What's your date of birth? - It's _____.

3. When you go abroad, you should _____.
   You mustn't _____.
   Try to _____.

Unit 03

Word Power!

Study this list of important new words and phrases in this unit. You can complete the list by adding more words that you learned.

Unit 3 で登場した重要語句のリストです。空所には、その他に新しく学んだ語句を自由に書き入れ、オリジナルのリストを作りましょう！

English	Japanese
☐ fill out (= fill in)	記入する
☐ arrival card	入国カード
☐ instructions	指示
☐ immigration	（空港などでの）入国審査、出入国管理
☐ documents	書類
☐ letter of enrollment	入学許可書
☐ bank statement	（貯金の）残高証明書
☐ politely	礼儀正しく
☐ carry-on luggage	機内持ち込み手荷物
☐ baggage claim	手荷物受取所
☐ customs	税関
☐ strict	厳格な
☐ arrivals area	到着ロビー
☐ nationality	国籍
☐ economy class syndrome	エコノミークラス症候群
☐ health insurance	健康保険
☐ occupation	職業
☐	
☐	
☐	
☐	
☐	
☐	
☐	

Unit

04 People

Unit Goals

● Introduce people   人を紹介する
● Talk about jobs and personality   仕事と人柄について話す
● Talk about present activities   現在の活動について話す

Warm-up

Look at Makiko's family tree and complete the sentences below.

マキコの家族の家系図を見て、下の文を完成しましょう。

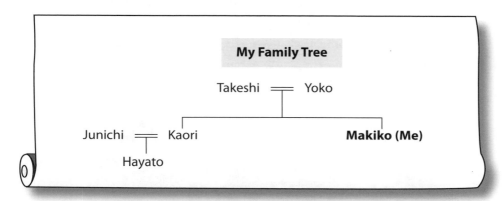

My mother is **1.**_____. My father is **2.**_____. I have an older

sister. Her name is **3.**_____. Junichi is her **4.**_____. Hayato is

my **5.**_____.

Listening 1: Short Talk

A ***Listen to Makiko talk about her family and answer these questions.***

マキコが自分の家族について話すのを聞いて、次の質問に答えましょう。

🎧 DL 19   ◎ CD 19

1. What's Takeshi's job?	He's a _____ teacher.
2. How old is Kaori?	She's _____ years old.
3. What does Junichi do in his free time?	He plays _____ games.

27

B *Look at the script and listen again. Fill in the blanks.*

スクリプトを見ながら音声をもう一度聞いて、空所を埋めましょう。

🎧 DL 19 💿 CD 19

My father's name is Takeshi. He is 54 years old, and he teaches history at a high school. He's a very **1.**_____ person, and he's rather quiet. He likes watching sports, especially rugby, and he enjoys eating out.

My mother's name is Yoko. She's 52 years old, and she works part-time in the local **2.**_____ . She's very creative and spends a lot of time making things by hand such as children's **3.**_____ .

My elder sister Kaori is 26 years old. She is married with one son and lives near our house. Her husband Junichi works for a software company as a programmer, and he enjoys playing computer games when he's at home. Their 1-year-old son Hayato is really **4.**_____ , so I often go over to their apartment to play with him.

Check with Your Partner!

With a partner, ask and answer these questions about the script.

上のスクリプトについて、ペアになって1〜3の質問をお互いにしてみましょう。

1. What's Takeshi like?

2. What does Yoko do in her free time?

3. What does Junichi do?

Key Phrases

This is … / He's … / Nice to meet you. / Please call me …

🔊 Patricia, this is Sam. He's on the football team.
- Nice to meet you. Please call me Pat.

She's a … / She's … / She works …

🔊 What does Erin do? - She's a nurse.
What's Fiona like? - She's very kind.
John works for a drug company. He works in a laboratory in Osaka.

She often … / She spends a lot of time …ing

🔊 My sister often goes to the movies.
My father spends a lot of time working in the garden.

Practice

Answer these questions using the words in the brackets.
[   ] 内の語句を使って、質問に答えましょう。

1. What does your sister do?   [an accountant.] [works — the city hall — York.]

_____

2. What's she like?   [serious.] [often studies — the library.]

_____

3. Who's this?   [my neighbor, John.] [loves — soccer.] [a fan — Liverpool FC.]

_____

Listening 2: Conversation

A *Here are some notes on Makiko's host family. Answer the questions below.*

以下はマキコのホストファミリーについてのメモです。下の質問に答えましょう。

Steve Benton
45 years old
French teacher
cheerful
rugby / Saturday

Katrina Benton
44 years old
housewife
friendly
volunteer work

Emma Benton
16 years old
part-time / bakery
positive
wants / dancer

1. What does Steve do?

He's _____.

2. What's Katrina like?

She's very _____.

3. What does Katrina like to do?

She likes to _____.

4. What's Emma's part-time job?

She works _____ a _____.

5. What does Emma want to be in the future?

She wants _____ a _____.

B *Listen to the conversation between Makiko and Katrina when they first meet at the airport, and circle T (true) or F (false) for the following sentences.*

マキコとカトリーナが初めて空港で会った時の会話を聞いて、次の文が正しければ T、誤っていれば F を丸で囲みましょう。

 DL 23　CD 23

1. Mrs. Benton says to call her Katrina.　　　　　　　　　　T　F

2. Katrina is going to take Emma to her dance class on the way home.　T　F

3. Steve couldn't come to the airport because he's working.　　T　F

Your Turn to Talk

A *Here are some notes on Makiko's friends. Complete the introductions below.*

以下はマキコの友達についてのメモです。下の紹介文を完成させましょう。

Jerry	**Maria**	**Your Friend**
19 years old	20 years old	_____
Taipei	Madrid	_____
studying / business English	studying / economics	_____
staying / host family	living / friends	_____
often / music	spends time / soccer	_____

1. _____ is Jerry. He's from _____. He is studying _____.
   He's staying with a _____. He often _____.
2. This _____ Maria _____ Madrid. She is majoring in _____.
   She's _____ with three _____. She spends a lot of
   time _____.

B *Now write information about one of your friends in the blanks above and draw a portrait of him/her in the box. Then practice making introductions with your partner.*

上の空所に、あなたの友達についての情報と似顔絵を書きましょう。それから、パートナーと友達を紹介する練習をしましょう。

Review
Key Phrases

Make sentences using the Key Phrases you learned in this unit.

このユニットで学んだ Key Phrases を使って文を作りましょう。

1. This is _____. He's _____ old. He works _____.
2. Mary is very _____. She often _____.
3. I spend a lot of time _____.

Word Power!

Study this list of important new words and phrases in this unit. You can complete the list by adding more words that you learned.

Unit 4 で登場した重要語句のリストです。空所には、その他に新しく学んだ語句を自由に書き入れ、オリジナルのリストを作りましょう！

English	Japanese
☐ personality	人柄
☐ family tree	家系図
☐ serious	真面目な
☐ rather	どちらかと言うと
☐ spend (time) doing	～して（時間を）過ごす
☐ What's he like?	彼はどんな人ですか。
☐ laboratory	研究所
☐ accountant	会計士
☐ do volunteer work	ボランティア活動をする
☐ positive	積極的な、前向きな
☐ on the way home	帰宅途中
☐ stay with a host family	ホストファミリーの家に滞在する ＝ホームステイをする
☐	
☐	
☐	
☐	
☐	
☐	
☐	
☐	
☐	
☐	
☐	

House Rules

Unit Goals

- Describe the location of things   物の場所を説明する
- Understand house rules   ハウスルール（家の決まり事）を理解する
- Understand how to use your room   部屋の使い方を理解する

Warm-up

Read the sentences below and label the furniture in this bedroom.

下の文を読んで、寝室の平面図上の①～⑥に家具の名前を書き入れましょう。

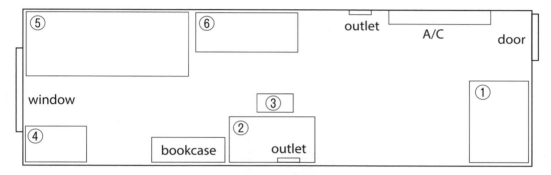

- **The bed** is in the corner by the window. **The armchair** is also near the window.
- When you come through the door, **the closet** is on your left in the corner.
- **The chest of drawers** is between the door and the bed.
- **The desk** and **chair** are along the wall opposite the chest of drawers.

Listening 1: Short Talk

A *Listen to this explanation about the bedroom and answer these questions.*

寝室についての説明を聞いて、次の質問に答えましょう。

🎧 DL 24   💿 CD 24

1. Where can you put your clothes?   In the _____ or the _____ of _____ .

2. Where can you hang your coat?   On the _____ of the _____ .

3. Where can you plug in a computer?   In the outlet under the _____ .

B *Look at the script and listen again. Fill in the blanks.*

スクリプトを見ながら音声をもう一度聞いて、空所を埋めましょう。

🎧 DL 24   💿 CD 24

Your bedroom is upstairs on the second floor, next to the bathroom. It has a large window with a view of the garden, so it's nice and **1.**_____.

You can put your clothes in the closet, which is very **2.**_____, or in the chest of drawers next to the bed. You can hang your winter coat on the back of the door.

For studying, you have a desk and chair, and you can put your books in the bookcase on the right. If you have a **3.**_____, you can plug it in under the desk. We have Wi-Fi, so you can use the internet whenever you like.

Finally, there's a very comfortable armchair. It's next to the window, so it's a good place to do some **4.**_____. If you need anything else, please ask me.

Check with Your Partner!

With a partner, ask and answer these questions about the script.

上のスクリプトについて、ペアになって1〜3の質問をお互いにしてみましょう。

1. What can you see from the bedroom window?

2. When can you use the internet?

3. Why is the armchair a good place for reading?

🎧 DL 25 ~ 27   ⊙ CD 25 ~ ⊙ CD 27

It's [in / on / by / near / between / under / above / next to / on the back of] ...

🔊 The towels are on the shelf in the cupboard under the stairs.
The new toothbrushes are in the cabinet above the sink.
They're between the shaving cream and the deodorant.

Please ... / Don't ... / Don't forget to ...

🔊 Please put your dirty clothes in the laundry basket in the utility room.
Don't leave dirty plates in the sink.
Don't forget to fold up your *futon* every morning and put it in the closet.

You can ...

🔊 You can put your textbooks in the bookcase.
You can change the temperature with this remote control.
I'll show you how to use it.

Practice

Answer these questions using the words in the brackets.

[　] 内の語句を使って、質問に答えましょう。

1. Where can I plug in my phone?　[next — the chest of drawers.]

You can plug it in the outlet _____

2. What time do I have to be home?　[forget — call — if — going to — late.]

Well, we don't have a curfew, but _____

3. Can I wash my clothes by myself?　[You — use the — machine — the kitchen.]

Sure. _____

Listening 2: Conversation

A *Read this memo about house rules from Makiko's host mother. Match each phrase on the left with one on the right.*

マキコのホストマザーが作ったハウスルールに関するメモを見て、左側（1～8）と右側（a～h）の語句をつなげましょう。

Benton Family Home – Homestay Rules

1. Keep your bedroom   **a.** a bath anytime.

2. I'll change the sheets   **b.** clean and tidy.

3. You can take   **c.** using the bathroom.

4. Clean up after   **d.** and pillowcases once a week.

5. Don't make a lot of noise   **e.** forget to call us.

6. If you don't want dinner,   **f.** homestay students.

7. There's no curfew for   **g.** after 10 o'clock at night.

8. If you're going to be late, don't   **h.** let me know before I start cooking.

1. (   )   **2.** (   )   **3.** (   )   **4.** (   )

5. (   )   **6.** (   )   **7.** (   )   **8.** (   )

B *Listen to the conversation between Makiko and her host mother, Katrina, about the memo, and circle T (true) or F (false) for the following sentences.*

マキコとホストマザーのカトリーナがメモについて話すのを聞いて、次の文が正しければ T、誤っていれば F を丸で囲みましょう。

🎧 DL 28   ⊙ CD 28

1. The Bentons have many rules for homestay students.   **T   F**

2. Katrina changes the sheets on Fridays.   **T   F**

3. Makiko says she will try to be quiet.   **T   F**

4. Katrina will worry if Makiko is late and she doesn't call.   **T   F**

Your Turn to Talk

A *Look at these rules for a Japanese house and choose the correct words in the brackets below.*

ある日本家庭のハウスルールを見て、下の文の（　　）内のうち正しいほうを選びましょう。

Please ...	· take your shoes off in the entrance hall · call if you are going to come home late · ·
Don't ...	· walk on *tatami* with your slippers on · wash yourself in the bathtub · ·
It's OK to ...	· use the internet whenever you want · take a shower whenever you want · ·

1. You (must / can) take your shoes off in the entrance hall.
2. You (mustn't / should) call if you are going to come home late.
3. You (mustn't / must) walk on *tatami* with your slippers on.
4. You (should / can) take a shower whenever you want.

B *What house rules would you have if a foreign student came to stay at your house? Add two more rules to each section above and explain them to your partner.*

あなたの家に留学生が滞在するとしたら、どんなハウスルールを決めますか。上の表のそれぞれの欄にルールを２つ書き加えて、パートナーに説明しましょう。

Make sentences using the Key Phrases you learned in this unit.

このユニットで学んだ Key Phrases を使って文を作りましょう。

1. There's no curfew, so I can _____ .
2. The _____ is in the cupboard above the sink _____ the kitchen.
3. My host mother worries a lot. She always says, "Don't _____
_____ ."

Word Power!

Study this list of important new words and phrases in this unit. You can complete the list by adding more words that you learned.

Unit 5 で登場した重要語句のリストです。空所には、その他に新しく学んだ語句を自由に書き入れ、オリジナルのリストを作りましょう！

English	Japanese
☐ closet	クローゼット
☐ chest of drawers	整理タンス
☐ (electric) outlet	（電気の）コンセント
☐ along the wall	壁に沿って
☐ plug in	プラグを差し込む
☐ whenever you like = any time you like	あなたがそうしたいときはいつでも
☐ anything else	他に何か
☐ cupboard	小さな戸棚、戸棚、食器棚
☐ cabinet	キャビネット、戸棚
☐ sink	洗面台
☐ utility room	家事室
☐ fold up (a *futon*)	（布団を）畳む
☐ curfew	門限
☐ tidy	整頓された
☐ pillowcase	枕カバー
☐ otherwise	もしそうでないなら
☐ for sure	必ず、きっと
☐ entrance hall	玄関
☐ with your slippers on	スリッパをはいて
☐ bathtub	湯船
☐	
☐	
☐	
☐	

Unit 06

Orientation

Unit Goals

● Explain using "If" sentences   If の文を使って説明する
● Talk about your schedule   時間割について話す
● Ask about meaning   意味を尋ねる

Warm-up

Read the following handout. Who is it for?

お知らせを読みましょう。誰のためのお知らせでしょうか。

Newton University
International Student Orientation

● **Schedule**

10:00 — 10:30	Registration for English course
10:30 — 11:30	Placement test in Room **1**(217 / 270)
11:30 — 1:00	Lunch
1:00 — 2:15	Campus tour

● **Things you need for registration**
  · your enrollment letter
  · your **2**(passport / student card)
  · a passport-sized photograph

● **Things you need for the placement test**
  · a pencil
  · an eraser
  · your **3**(passport / student card)

Listening 1: Short Talk

A *Listen to the teacher's talk and choose the correct answers in the brackets above.*

先生の説明を聞いて、上の 1 〜 3 の（   ）内のうち正しいほうを選びましょう。

 DL 29   CD 29

39

B Look at the script and listen again. Fill in the blanks.

スクリプトを見ながら音声をもう一度聞いて、空所を埋めましょう。

🎧 DL 29   💿 CD 29

Good morning, everybody! Welcome to Newton University! I'm David Hill from the English Language Center.

First of all today, you are going to **1.** _____ for your English course, and then you will have a **2.** _____ test. You will need the following things for registration: your enrollment letter, your passport, and a passport-sized photograph. If you don't have these things, please speak to me. OK?

After you have registered, please go to Room 217 for the placement test, which **3.** _____ at 10:30. By the way, "217" means the 7th room on the 1st floor in Building 2. For the placement test, you will need a pencil, an eraser, and the student card you receive at registration. Again, if you have any **4.** _____ about the test, please see me.

Check with Your Partner!

With a partner, ask and answer these questions about the script.

上のスクリプトについて、ペアになって１～３の質問をお互いにしてみましょう。

1. What time does the placement test begin?
2. What does "217" mean?
3. What should students do if they have any questions about the test?

 DL 30 ~ 32   CD 30 ~ CD 32

Key Phrases

If ..., ...

If you have any questions about the test, please see me.

If you are ill, you can take the test next week.

If you are late for the test, you will not be able to enter the test room.

It begins / starts / finishes / ends at ...

The placement test begins at 10:30.

The campus tour finishes at 2:15.

It means ... / It stands for ...

What does "217" mean?

- It means the 7th room on the 1st floor in Building 2.

"L & S" on the schedule means Listening and Speaking class.

"MC" stands for Multimedia Center.

Practice

Answer these questions using the words in the brackets.

[   ] 内の語句を使って、質問に答えましょう。

1. What can you see if you visit New York?   [If you — New York, — the Empire State Building.]

_____

2. What time is your afternoon class?   [starts — 2:00 — finishes — 2:50.]

_____

3. What does "LL" stand for?   [It — Language Laboratory.]

_____

Listening 2: Conversation

A *Look at Kenta's schedule and answer the questions below.*

ケンタの時間割を見て、下の質問に答えましょう。

	Monday	Tuesday	Wednesday	Thursday	Friday
9:00 – 10:30	Listening & Speaking (L & S)　118	L & S　118	L & S　118	L & S　118	L & S　118
10:45 – 12:15	Reading & Writing (R & W)　231	R & W　231	R & W　231	R & W　231	R & W　231
Lunch					
1:30 – 2:30	Multimedia Center **	Tutoring *	Multimedia Center **	Tutoring *	Cultural Trip or Activity **
2:40 – 3:40		Self-Access Center **		Self-Access Center **	

* By appointment　　** Optional

1. If he wants to, what can Kenta join on Friday afternoon?

   He can _____ a _____.

2. When does the first class begin each day? And when does it end?

   It begins at _____ and ends _____.

3. What does Kenta have just before lunch on Monday?

   He has _____.

4. "118" means the 8th room on the 1st floor in Building 1. What does "231" mean?

   It means _____.

B *Listen to the conversation between Kenta and his teacher about the schedule and circle T (true) or F (false) for the following sentences.*

ケンタと先生が時間割について話すのを聞いて、次の文が正しければ T、誤っていれば F を丸で囲みましょう。

🎧 DL 33　　💿 CD 33

1. If Kenta is more than 5 minutes late for class, he will be absent.　　**T　F**

2. "Tutoring" means meeting your tutor in his or her home.　　**T　F**

3. If Kenta wants to study by himself, he can go to the Health Center.　　**T　F**

Your Turn to Talk

A *Look at your schedule and fill in the blanks in the sentences below.*

これはあなたの時間割です。下の文の空所を埋めましょう。

	Monday	Tuesday	Wednesday	Thursday	Friday
9:00 – 10:30	Speaking	Listening	Speaking		
10:45 – 12:15		Reading		Listening	Reading
Lunch					
1:30 – 2:30		Tutoring *			Cultural Trip
2:40 – 3:40	Self-Access Center **		Multimedia Center **	Writing	

* By appointment   ** Optional

1. I have Speaking classes on Monday and _____. They start at 9:00 and end at _____ .

2. I also have _____ classes twice a week on Tuesday and Thursday. My Thursday class begins at _____ .

3. If I have time, I can go to the _____ on Monday afternoon. Two asterisks (**) means that self-access study is _____ .

B *Put the following courses into your schedule and then talk about it with a partner. Try to make four sentences.*

次の科目を時間割の空いているコマに入れてから、パートナーとその時間割について話しましょう。4つの文を作ってみましょう。

English Grammar (x2)   Writing (x2)   Area Studies **   TOEFL Preparation

Review
Key Phrases

Make sentences using the Key Phrases you learned in this unit.

このユニットで学んだ Key Phrases を使って文を作りましょう。

1. If _____ , I will fail my class.
2. My _____ class begins at _____ and ends at _____ .
3. "MC" doesn't mean "multiple choice." It _____ Multimedia Center.

Word Power!

Study this list of important new words and phrases in this unit. You can complete the list by adding more words that you learned.

Unit 6 で登場した重要語句のリストです。空所には、その他に新しく学んだ語句を自由に書き入れ、オリジナルのリストを作りましょう！

English	Japanese
☐ schedule	時間割
☐ registration	登録
☐ placement test	クラス分けテスト
☐ first of all	まず最初に
☐ register	登録する
☐ stands for	〜を表す
☐ multimedia center	マルチメディアセンター
☐ tutoring	個人指導
☐ self-access center	自習室
☐ on time	時間通りに
☐ absent	欠席の
☐ study materials	学習教材
☐ asterisk	星印 (*)
☐ area studies	地域研究
☐	
☐	
☐	
☐	
☐	
☐	
☐	
☐	
☐	
☐	

Unit 07

First Lesson Day

Unit Goals

- Talk about self-study activities 　　自習活動について話す
- Understand directions 　　　　　　道案内を理解する
- Talk about location 　　　　　　　場所について話す

Warm-up

Read this explanation of activities offered by the English Language Center (ELC). Check the activity that interests you most.

これは、English Language Center (ELC) が提供する活動についての説明です。あなたが一番興味のある活動にチェック (☑) してみましょう。

Newton University English Language Center
Self-Study Activities – "Just Do It!"

☐ **Multimedia Center**

Choose from our exciting collection of movies and TV programs. We have 12 booths with DVD and Blu-ray disc players.

☐ **Self-Access Center**

Improve your grammar, vocabulary, and reading skills. We have a large collection of graded readers and reading cards.

☐ **ELC Social Club**

Join events and activities with ELC students from many different countries.

Listening 1: Short Talk

A *Listen to the talk about ELC activities and answer these questions.*

ELC の活動についての話を聞いて、次の質問に答えましょう。

🎧 DL 34　💿 CD 34

1. Are the activities compulsory or optional?　　They're _____.
2. When is this week's ELC Social Club activity?　It's on _____.
3. What can you do in Wellington Park?　　　　You can _____.

B *Look at the script and listen again. Fill in the blanks.*

スクリプトを見ながら音声をもう一度聞いて、空所を埋めましょう。

🎧 DL 34　◉ CD34

If you want to learn English well, just studying in class is not **1.** _____. You also have to study by yourself.

Here at the ELC, when you have free time, you can go to the Multimedia Center to watch movies and TV programs. Also, you can study by yourself in the Self-Access Center to **2.** _____ your reading, vocabulary, and grammar.

In addition, you can join an ELC Social Club activity and speak English with other students. If you look at the club's website, you'll see there is one event this week. On Saturday, you can play futsal in Wellington Park. Do you know where the park is? Well, just go **3.** _____ along Pine Street for about 200 yards from the university, and you'll see the park on the **4.** _____. Everybody is welcome!

Check with Your Partner!

With a partner, ask and answer these questions about the script.

上のスクリプトについて、ペアになって1〜3の質問をお互いにしてみましょう。

1. Why do students go to the Multimedia Center?

2. How do you get to Wellington Park? (*Hint: Go …*)

3. Is the park on the right or on the left?

46

DL 35 ~ 37   CD 35 ~ CD 37

Key Phrases

You can go to [a place] to [do something] ...

🔊 You can go to the Multimedia Center to watch a TV program.
Why did you go to Wellington Park?
- I went there to play futsal.

Go [down/up/along] ... and turn ...

🔊 Do you know the way to the swimming pool?
- Yes. Go down High Street to the second traffic light and turn right.
Do you know the way to the bus station?
- Yes. Go along this street as far as McDonald's and turn left.

It's ...yards on the [left/right]. / It's [next to/opposite/between] ...

🔊 The bakery is about 50 yards on the left, next to a boutique.
It's between a bar and a coffee shop. It's opposite a dry cleaner's.
It's on the corner of High Street and Market Street.

Practice

Answer these questions using the words in the brackets.
[   ] 内の語句を使って、質問に答えましょう。

1. What can you do in the Multimedia Center?   [You can — there to watch — or — .]

_____

2. Can you tell me the way to Starbucks?
                    [Go — Baker Street — the second traffic light and — left.]

Sure. _____

3. Where is the dry cleaner's?   [It's 200 yards — the right — a bar — a pet shop.]

_____

47

Listening 2: Conversation

A *Makiko is going to the English Language Center for the first time by herself. Look at the map and answer the questions below.*

マキコは初めて一人で English Language Center に行くつもりです。地図を見て、下の質問に答えましょう。

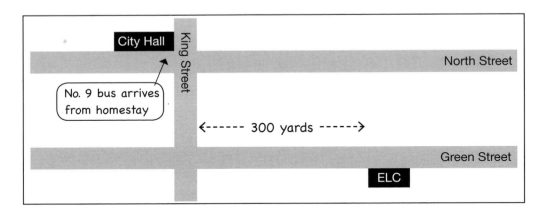

1. Where does the No. 9 bus stop?

It _____ in front of _____ .

2. Where is the ELC?

It's on _____ Street about _____ from King Street.

3. How can you get from city hall to the ELC?

Walk down _____ Street as far as _____ Street and turn _____ . The ELC is on the _____-hand side.

B *Listen to the conversation between Makiko and her host mother just before Makiko leaves home and circle T (true) or F (false) for the following sentences.*

家を出る直前のマキコとホストマザーの会話を聞いて、次の文が正しければ T、誤っていれば F を丸で囲みましょう。

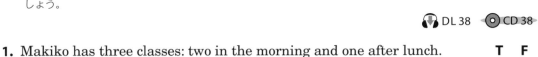

1. Makiko has three classes: two in the morning and one after lunch.   **T**   **F**

2. She'll probably get home after dinnertime.   **T**   **F**

3. She knows the way to the ELC.   **T**   **F**

4. The homestay address and telephone number are on a card in her purse.   **T**   **F**

Your Turn to Talk

A *Look at the map and complete the sentences below to give directions from the post office to the bank, the butcher, and the bookstore.*

地図を見て、郵便局から 1. 銀行、2. 精肉店、3. 書店へ行く道順を説明する文を完成させましょう。

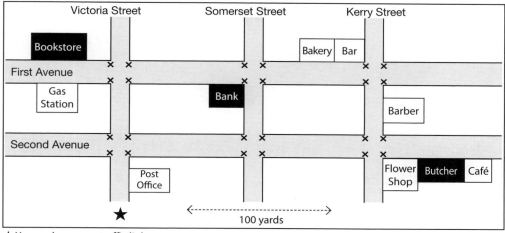

★ You are here. ✕ = traffic lights

1. Walk down Victoria Street as far as the _____ traffic light and turn right. The bank is on the right, on the _____ of First Avenue and Somerset Street.

2. Just turn _____ at the first traffic light and walk about 200 yards. The butcher is _____ the right between a café and a flower shop.

3. Go straight ahead _____ the second traffic light and turn left. The bookstore is on the right-hand side of First Avenue, _____ a gas station.

B *Work with a partner. Ask for and give directions to two places each on the map.*

地図上にある場所のうち、2つを選びましょう。ペアになって、一人は選んだ場所への行き方を尋ね、もう一人はそれに答えましょう。その後、役割を交代して同じように会話しましょう。

e.g. "Do you know the way to the …?" "Yes. …"

Make sentences using the Key Phrases you learned in this unit.

このユニットで学んだ Key Phrases を使って文を作りましょう。

1. Makiko can _____ to City Stadium _____ watch a baseball game _____ her classmates.

2. Go _____ this street as _____ as the supermarket and _____ left.

3. The factory is _____ 100 yards down the street _____ the right. It's on the _____ of Cromwell Street and Walton Road.

49

Word Power!

Study this list of important new words and phrases in this unit. You can complete the list by adding more words that you learned.

Unit 7 で登場した重要語句のリストです。空所には、その他に新しく学んだ語句を自由に書き入れ、オリジナルのリストを作りましょう！

	English	Japanese
☐	self-study	自習
☐	directions	行き方、方角
☐	location	場所
☐	offer	提供する
☐	booth	仕切り席
☐	improve	向上させる
☐	graded readers	学習到達度別の読み物
☐	compulsory	必修の
☐	optional	選択が自由の
☐	go down/up/along	〜に沿って行く
☐	traffic light	交通信号
☐	as far as	〜まで
☐	butcher	肉屋
☐		
☐		
☐		
☐		
☐		
☐		
☐		
☐		
☐		
☐		
☐		

Unit Goals

- Say what you want to do   やりたいことを伝える
- Express necessity   必要性を説明する
- Express obligation   義務を説明する

Warm-up

Look at these pictures of activities in Auckland. Match each activity (A-C) with a name from the box below.

以下は、オークランドでできるアクティビティです。 A 〜 C の写真に合う語句を下から選んで書き入れましょう。

Language Center Activities in February

A. [   ]   **B.** [   ]   **C.** [   ]

Feb. **1**(1st / 4th)
* one-day trip

Feb. **2**(9th / 18th)
* half-day trip

On **3**(Wednesday / Thursday)
* from 3:30 -5:00

Come join us for these exciting activities in Auckland!

Conversation Club   Waiheke Island   Muriwai Beach Horse Trek

Listening 1: Short Talk

A *Listen to this presentation about the three activities and choose the correct days in the brackets above.*

3つのアクティビティに関する説明を聞いて、上の 1 〜 3 の (   ) 内のうち正しいほうの日付を選びましょう。

 DL 39   CD 39

B *Look at the script and listen again. Fill in the blanks.*

スクリプトを見ながら音声をもう一度聞いて、空所を埋めましょう。

🎧 DL 39 💿 CD 39

Now, this slide shows the Language Center's activities in February. First, on **1.**_____, February 4th, we have a one-day trip to Waiheke Island. If you want to join this trip, please meet at Auckland Ferry Terminal at 9:00 a.m. On Waiheke Island, you can visit the beautiful Oneroa Beach and also a nearby **2.**_____. The total cost will be about 45 dollars.

Next, on February 18th, there is a half-day trip to Muriwai Beach for horse trekking. This is suitable for beginners and costs **3.**_____ dollars. You need to wear long trousers and sneakers. If you would like to join this activity, you have to sign your name on the noticeboard before February 14th.

Finally, as **4.**_____, the Conversation Club will hold a meeting on Wednesday afternoon from 3:30 to 5:00.

Check with Your Partner!

With a partner, ask and answer these questions about the script.

上のスクリプトについて、ペアになって1〜3の質問をお互いにしてみましょう。

1. If you want to go to Waiheke Island, where do you have to meet?
2. What do you need to wear for horse trekking?
3. If you would like to go horse trekking, what do you have to do before February 14th?

 DL 40 ~ 42 CD 40 ~ CD 42

Key Phrases

I want to ... / I would like to ...

I want to take a trip around Australia after my course finishes.
Would you like to go to the beach next Sunday?
- Thanks, I'd love to.
- I'm sorry, I can't. I have to go to driving school.

I need to ...

I need to earn some money before I can study abroad.
You don't need to make a reservation. It's not necessary.

You have to ...

You have to make a reservation if you want to go horseback riding.
You have to stop at a red light. It's dangerous if you don't. In fact, you must stop. It's the law.

Practice

Answer these questions using the words in the brackets.
[   ] 内の語句を使って、質問に答えましょう。

1. Would you like to have coffee with us?   [sorry — can't.] [have to — my part-time job.]

_____

2. What do you need to do before you go abroad?   [I — get a visa and — insurance.]

_____

3. Do you want to take a trip this summer?   [Yes, I — go surfing — Hawaii.]

_____

Listening 2: Conversation

A *Look at this notice about an activity. Where and when are the students going to go?*

ELC のアクティビティについての掲示を見て、下の質問に答えましょう。学生はどこに、いつ行く予定でしょうか。

North Adelaide College – English Language Center

Saturday, March 6th, Glenelg Beach

Tram from King William Street

Volleyball, Badminton, Swimming

Meeting time and place: 1 p.m., in front of the ELC

1. Where are they going to go?   They are _____.

2. When are they going to go?   They are _____.

3. How are they going to get there?   They are _____.

B *Listen to the conversation between Ikuko from Japan and Lee from Taiwan, and circle T (true) or F (false) for the following sentences.*

日本出身のイクコと台湾出身のリーの会話を聞いて、次の文が正しければ T、誤っていれば F を丸で囲みましょう。

🎧 DL 43   💿 CD 43

1. Ikuko wants to go to Glenelg Beach with Lee.   T   F

2. At the beach, they are going to play some games first.   T   F

3. There are only a few shops near the beach.   T   F

4. They need to bring fans because it's hot at the beach.   T   F

5. Ikuko will probably go shopping before going to the beach.   T   F

Your Turn to Talk

A *Look at this chart about activities at Duncan College and complete the sentences below. Ken has checked (☑) the one he wants to join.*

これは、Duncan College でのアクティビティに関する案内です。ケンは、参加したい活動にチェック（☑）をしました。ケンの予定について、下の文を完成させましょう。

Duncan College, Vancouver Island
August English Language Program – Activities

	Date	Activity	Details	You need ...
☐	Aug 10	Whale Watching	View the whales in the seas around Vancouver Island	a swimsuit
☐	Aug 16-18	Visit Vancouver	Have two days' free time in Vancouver	an overnight bag
☐	Aug 21	The ELC International Food Night	Try many kinds of food prepared by students from many different countries	a good appetite
☑	Aug 24	Hiking in Goldstream Park	Enjoy the fresh air and beautiful scenery	hiking shoes, a rain jacket

On August 24th, Ken wants to _____.

There, he can _____.

He needs to bring _____.

B *Now choose two activities you want to do and tell your partner about them.*

あなたが参加したいアクティビティを2つ選び、上の文を参考にしてパートナーに伝えましょう。

Review Key Phrases

Make sentences using the Key Phrases you learned in this unit.

このユニットで学んだ Key Phrases を使って文を作りましょう。

I would like to visit _____ because I want to _____

_____. I also want to _____. Before

I go there, I need to _____ and I have to

_____.

Word Power!

Study this list of important new words and phrases in this unit. You can complete the list by adding more words that you learned.

Unit 8 で登場した重要語句のリストです。空所には、その他に新しく学んだ語句を自由に書き入れ、オリジナルのリストを作りましょう！

English	Japanese
☐ trek	トレッキング
☐ nearby	近くの
☐ winery	ぶどう酒醸造所、ワイナリー
☐ trousers (= pants)	ズボン
☐ noticeboard	掲示板
☐ earn	（お金を）稼ぐ
☐ reservation	予約
☐ horseback riding (= horse riding)	乗馬
☐ tram	路面電車
☐ Sounds good!	いいですね！
☐ sunscreen	日焼け止めクリーム
☐ details	詳細
☐ whale	クジラ
☐ overnight bag	一泊旅行用カバン
☐ appetite	食欲
☐ scenery	景色、風景
☐	
☐	
☐	
☐	
☐	
☐	
☐	
☐	

Unit 09

Housework

Unit Goals

● Make requests 依頼する
● Ask permission 許可を求める
● Offer to help 手伝いを申し出る

Warm-up

Look at this housework list. Choose an appropriate word for each blank from the box below.

家事に関するリストを見て、1~6 の空所に入る単語を下から選んで書き入れましょう。

Common household jobs in the U.S.

Women

· ¹(   ) meals
· Cleaning the ²(   )
· Doing the ³(   )

Men

· Helping ⁴(   ) meals
· ⁵(   ) in the garden
· ⁶(   ) things in the house

repairing	preparing	working	house	laundry	with

Listening 1: Short Talk

A *Listen to this talk about housework in the U.S. and answer these questions.*

アメリカの家事事情についての話を聞いて、次の質問に答えましょう。

🎧 DL 44　◉ CD 44

1. How long does the average woman spend on housework in the U.S.?
She spends _____ hours _____ minutes a day.

2. How long does the average man spend on housework in the U.S.?
He spends _____ hour _____ minutes a day.

3. Do children help with housework? _____, they _____.

B *Look at the script and listen again. Fill in the blanks.*

スクリプトを見ながら音声をもう一度聞いて、空所を埋めましょう。

🎧 DL 44   💿 CD 44

In English-speaking countries, all **1.**_____ of the family usually help with housework. In America, for example, the average woman spends 2 hours 15 minutes on housework every day. The **2.**_____ man does less than a woman, but he still spends about 1 hour 25 minutes a day on housework.

The most common jobs for women are preparing meals, cleaning the house, and doing the laundry, in that order. The most common jobs for men are helping with meals, working in the **3.**_____, and repairing things in the house. Even children have to do some chores, such as cleaning their rooms or washing the dishes.

When students do homestay, they should **4.**_____ a little as well. So don't forget to ask: "Can I help you?"

Check with Your Partner!

With a partner, ask and answer these questions about the script.

上のスクリプトについて、ペアになって 1〜3 の質問をお互いにしてみましょう。

1. What is the most common household job for women in the U.S.?
2. Do American men repair things in the house?
3. What kind of housework do American children sometimes do?

🎧 DL 45 ~ 47 ⊙ CD 45 ~ ⊙ CD 47

Could you ...? (request) - Yes, sure. / Yes, of course.

📢 Could you please close the windows before you go to bed?
Could you put the butter in the refrigerator?

Can I ...? (asking permission) - Yes, sure. / Yes, of course.

📢 Can I borrow your bicycle to go to the supermarket?
Could I borrow your bicycle? *(more polite than "Can I ...?")*

Shall I ... ? (offering to help) - Oh, yes, please.

📢 Shall I peel the potatoes?
Shall I set the table?
Can I help you? *(general way to offer help)*

Practice

Make questions for the following situations using the words in the brackets.
[   ] 内の語句を使って、次の状況にあった質問文を作りましょう。

1. You want someone to help with cooking.   [Could — cut the vegetables?]

_____

2. You want to do the laundry.   [use the — machine?]

_____

3. You want to help your host mother with cleaning.   [Shall — the living room?]

_____

59

Listening 2: Conversation

A *Look at the illustrations showing the locations of electric appliances, and put the correct prepositions from the box in the sentences below.*

家電製品の場所を表すイラストを見て、会話の空所に入る前置詞を下から選んで書き入れましょう。

1. Iron   **2.** Hairdryer   **3.** Blender

1. A: Can I use the iron?

    B: Yes, sure. It's _____ the closet _____ the laundry room.

2. A: Do you know where the hairdryer is?

    B: Yes, it's _____ the drawer next _____ the bathroom sink.

3. A: Is it OK if I use the blender?

    B: Yes, of course. It's _____ the shelf _____ the kitchen sink.

above	in	in	in	on	to

B *Listen to the conversation between Makiko and Katrina, her host mother, and circle T (true) or F (false) for the following sentences.*

マキコとホストマザーのカトリーナとの会話を聞いて、次の文が正しければ T、誤っていれば F を丸で囲みましょう。

DL 48   CD 48

1. Makiko wants to iron some shirts.   **T   F**

2. The iron is in a closet in the kitchen.   **T   F**

3. Katrina shows Makiko how to use the iron.   **T   F**

4. Makiko thinks it's difficult to use the iron.   **T   F**

Your Turn to Talk

A *Read this to-do list written by your host mother and fill in the blanks using the words below.*

ホストマザーの書いた「やることリスト」を読んで、1～5に入る単語を下から選んで書き入れましょう。

☐ vacuum the living room ☐ 2._____ the kitchen floor
☐ wash the 1._____ ☐ mow the 3._____
☐ clean the windows ☐ 4._____ the light bulb in the bathroom
☐ go grocery shopping ☐ take out the 5._____
☐ ☐
☐ ☐

lawn   change   blankets   sweep   trash

B *Work with your partner and add four more things to do in the list. Then practice the conversation below.*

ペアになって、上のリストにあと4つ書き足しましょう。その後、次のように会話を練習しましょう。

 DL 49   CD 49

You: Can I help you?
Host parent: Oh, yes, please. That's very kind of you.
You: What shall I do?
Host parent: Well, could you *vacuum the living room*?
You: Sure. Just leave it to me. Shall I *clean the windows* too?
Host parent: No, I'll do that later. Thanks.

Review
Key
Phrases

Make sentences using the Key Phrases you learned in this unit.

このユニットで学んだ Key Phrases を使って文を作りましょう。

1. A: You look tired, Mrs. Smith. _____ I cook dinner?
   B: Oh, _____ you.
2. A: I feel very hot. _____ I open the _____ ?   B: Yes, sure.
3. A: Mmm… this looks delicious. _____ you pass the salt, _____ ?
   B: Yes, sure. Here you _____ .

Word Power!

Study this list of important new words and phrases in this unit. You can complete the list by adding more words that you learned.

Unit 9 で登場した重要語句のリストです。空所には、その他に新しく学んだ語句を自由に書き入れ、オリジナルのリストを作りましょう！

English	Japanese
☐ housework / household jobs	家事
☐ common	一般的な
☐ do the laundry	洗濯をする
☐ repair	修繕する
☐ average	平均的な
☐ in that order	その順番で
☐ chores	（家庭の）雑仕事、家事
☐ wash the dishes	（食後の）皿洗いをする
☐ refrigerator (fridge)	冷蔵庫
☐ polite	丁寧な、礼儀正しい
☐ peel	皮をむく
☐ set the table	食卓の用意をする
☐ ironing board	アイロン台
☐ blanket	毛布
☐ grocery, groceries	食料品
☐ sweep	（ほうきなどで）掃く、掃除する
☐ mow the lawn	芝を刈る
☐ leave it to me	それは私に任せてください
☐	
☐	
☐	
☐	
☐	
☐	

Unit 10

Food and Drink

Unit Goals

- Describe food and drink   飲食物について説明する
- Ask for and offer food   食べ物を頼んだり、提供したりする
- Give your impression of food   食べ物の感想を言う

Warm-up

Look at these pictures of special kinds of food and drink from English-speaking countries and match each one with a description below.

英語圏の独特な飲食物の写真を見て、下の説明と組み合わせましょう。

· **California roll** is a kind of sushi containing cucumber, crab meat, and avocado. Sushi was brought to the U.S. by Japanese immigrants.   (   )
· **A flat white** is a kind of coffee in Australia. It is made with espresso and frothy milk. Coffee culture was brought to Australia by Italian immigrants.   (   )
· **Roast lamb** is a very popular dish in New Zealand. Sheep were brought to New Zealand by British immigrants.   (   )

Listening 1: Short Talk

A *Listen to this talk about food and drink in English-speaking countries and answer these questions.*

英語圏の飲食物についての話を聞いて、次の質問に答えましょう。

🎧 DL 50   💿 CD 50

1. Which three countries are famous for food?

France, _____, and _____.

2. Does California roll look like Japanese sushi?

_____. It looks a lot _____.

B *Look at the script and listen again. Fill in the blanks.*

スクリプトを見ながら音声をもう一度聞いて、空所を埋めましょう。

🎧 DL 50　◎ CD 50

If you ask people "Which countries are famous for food?", they usually say France or Italy or China. They never say Britain or Canada or Australia. In fact, if you ask people their **1.**_____ of British food, they'll probably say "It's not very **2.**_____." However, if you visit English-speaking countries, you will find many kinds of interesting food and drink because there are so many immigrants.

Italian immigrants had a very strong **3.**_____ on Australia's coffee culture. A popular coffee drink there is called a "flat white." It's made with espresso and frothy milk. Sushi was brought to the U.S. by Japanese immigrants, and a California roll is a **4.**_____ kind of sushi in America. It's made with cucumber, crab meat, and avocado. It looks a lot different from traditional Japanese sushi, but it tastes really good.

Check with Your Partner!

With a partner, ask and answer these questions about the script.

上のスクリプトについて、ペアになって1〜3の質問をお互いにしてみましょう。

1. Why are there many kinds of interesting food in English-speaking countries?

2. What is a flat white made with?

3. How does a California roll taste?

Key Phrases

It's a kind of ... / It's made with ... / It contains ...

📢) *Daifuku-mochi* is a kind of rice cake. It's made with rice flour and sugar. It contains sweet bean paste.
Yogurt is made <u>from</u> milk.
The bread basket is made <u>of</u> bamboo.

Would you like ...?

📢) Would you like dessert? - Yes, please. I'd like some pie.
Would you like something to drink? - No, thanks.

It looks / tastes / smells ...

📢) That bread looks nice. And it smells delicious.
It tastes nice. It tastes <u>like</u> melon. It smells <u>like</u> melon too.

Practice

Answer these questions using the words in the brackets.

[   ] 内の語句を使って、質問に答えましょう。

1. What's *poutine*?   [made — French fries, cheese — gravy.]

It's a Canadian dish from Quebec. _____

2. What would you like?   [chicken curry — a green salad.]

_____

3. Is the fruit good?   [Yes, — delicious.] [tastes — mango.]

_____

A *Look at these pictures and descriptions of dinner at a host family's house. Answer the questions below.*

ホームステイ先でのディナーの写真と説明を見て、下の質問に答えましょう。

Lancashire Hotpot: Lamb and onion topped with sliced potatoes and baked in the oven

Garden Salad: Iceberg lettuce with tomatoes, carrot, and green pepper

Bakewell Tart: Pastry covered with jam, frangipane, and almond flakes

(Note: Frangipane is made from butter, sugar, eggs, and ground almonds.)

1. What does Lancashire hotpot contain?

It _____.

2. What's a garden salad made with?

It _____.

3. Would you like some Bakewell tart?

Yes, _____. It looks _____.

B *Listen to the conversations between Saki and her host father at dinner, and circle T (true) or F (false) for the following sentences.*

夕食時のサキとホストファーザーの会話を聞いて、次の文が正しければT、誤っていればFを丸で囲みましょう。

🎧 DL 54, 55   ⊙ CD 54   ⊙ CD 55

1. Saki praises the hotpot. She says it tastes really good. **T F**

2. Saki's host father grew the lettuce in his garden. **T F**

3. Saki doesn't have any ice cream because she's on a diet. **T F**

Your Turn to Talk

A *Read this Japanese restaurant menu and fill in the blanks with the items below.*

日本食レストランのメニューを読んで、1～4に入るものを下から選んで書き入れましょう。

Food		
1.	— Chinese-style noodles in soup	$ 9.00
Omusubi	— a rice ball	$ 1.50
2.	— bread containing sweet bean paste	$ 2.50
3.	— a kind of sponge cake	$ 3.00

Drinks				
Ramune	— a kind of lemonade	$ 1.60	**4.** — barley tea	$ 1.50
Yakult	— a kind of yogurt drink	$ 0.80		

Kasutera   *Ramen*   *Anpan*   *Mugicha*

B *Now practice conversations using items on the menu with a partner.*

ペアになって、メニューにあるアイテムを使って次のように会話を練習しましょう。

🎧 DL 56   ◎ CD 56

A: Would you like something to *eat / drink*?

B: Yes, I'm so hungry. What's on the menu?

A: Well, they have *ramen*.

B: *Ramen*? What's that?

A: It's *Chinese-style noodles in soup*.

B: OK. I'll try it.

…

A: Do you like it?

B: Yes, it tastes *good*.

Review Key Phrases

Make sentences using the Key Phrases you learned in this unit.

このユニットで学んだ Key Phrases を使って文を作りましょう。

1. *Okonomiyaki* is a Japanese _____. It's made with _____.

2. Would _____ something to drink?

  - Yes, please. Could I have a glass of _____?

3. Kimchi is a famous _____ dish. It tastes _____.

Word Power!

Study this list of important new words and phrases in this unit. You can complete the list by adding more words that you learned.

Unit 10 で登場した重要語句のリストです。空所には、その他に新しく学んだ語句を自由に書き入れ、オリジナルのリストを作りましょう！

English	Japanese
☐ immigrant	移民
☐ frothy	泡状の
☐ lamb	子羊の肉
☐ in fact	事実
☐ rice flour	米粉
☐ sweet bean paste	あんこ
☐ gravy	グレービーソース（肉汁から作るソース）
☐ Lancashire	ランカシャー（イングランド北西部の州）
☐ tart	タルト
☐ pastry	（小麦粉でできた）焼き菓子の生地
☐ flakes	薄片
☐ ground almonds	アーモンド粉
☐ praise	ほめる
☐ lose weight	体重を減らす
☐ barley	大麦
☐	
☐	
☐	
☐	
☐	
☐	
☐	
☐	
☐	

Unit 11

Money and Shopping

Unit Goals

- Shop for clothes　　　　　　服を買う
- Compare shopping items　　　商品を比較する
- Talk about size　　　　　　　サイズについて話す

Warm-up

Match a word on the left with a description on the right.

1〜5のお金に関する語句と a〜e の説明を結びつけましょう。

Money Vocabulary

1. bank account
2. international debit card
3. exchange rate
4. cash
5. ATM

a. bills and coins
b. automated teller machine
c. where you can keep your money
d. for example, the value of one U.S. dollar in yen
e. card that you can use to get money from a cash machine when you are abroad

---

1. (　)　　**2.** (　)　　**3.** (　)　　**4.** (　)　　**5.** (　)

Listing 1: Short Talk

A *Listen to Kenta's talk about how he dealt with money when he went abroad last year, and then answer these questions.*

ケンタが去年外国に行ったときにどのようにお金を扱ったかについて話すのを聞いて、次の質問に答えましょう。

 DL 57　　CD 57

1. What did Kenta do before going to New Zealand?

He opened an account at ＿＿＿＿＿＿＿ Bank.

2. What cards did he carry?

He carried an international ＿＿＿＿＿＿＿ card and a ＿＿＿＿＿＿＿.

3. What kind of money did he take with him to New Zealand?

He took some ＿＿＿＿＿＿＿.

B *Look at the script and listen again. Fill in the blanks.*

スクリプトを見ながら音声をもう一度聞いて、空所を埋めましょう。

🎧 DL 57   💿 CD 57

Last year I studied abroad for six months in New Zealand. Before going abroad, I opened a bank account at Iroha Bank. Why? Well, because Iroha Bank has an international debit card. My **1.** _____ put money in my bank account in Japan, and I used the debit card to get New Zealand dollars from an ATM in Wellington.

In addition, I had a credit card. It's more convenient to do online shopping and to make travel **2.** _____ with a credit card. I also used it when I bought something expensive.

As for cash, I took some Japanese yen from Japan, and at Wellington Airport, I changed just **3.** _____ for my first few days in New Zealand. Actually, you shouldn't carry **4.** _____ much cash. You might lose it! Just carry enough for your daily needs.

Check with Your Partner!

With a partner, ask and answer these questions about the script.

上のスクリプトについて、ペアになって1～3の質問をお互いにしてみましょう。

1. Why did Kenta choose Iroha Bank?

2. What's the advantage of a credit card?

3. What's Kenta's advice about carrying cash? What does he say?

 DL 58 ~ 60   CD 58 ~ CD 60

Key Phrases

I'm looking for …

🔊 Can I help you? Are you looking for anything special?
-Yes, I'm looking for a summer sweater. I think I'm a medium.
I'm looking for an ATM. I need to get some cash.

…er / more …

🔊 I'd like a smaller shirt.
I'm looking for a more colorful one.
I'd like something warmer and more fashionable.

It's too … / It's not … enough.

🔊 This suitcase is too expensive for me. And it's not big enough.
I spent too <u>much</u> money. I bought too <u>many</u> souvenirs.

Practice

Answer these questions using the words in the brackets.

[   ] 内の語句を使って、質問に答えましょう。

1. Can I help you?   [looking — a tennis racket.] [a beginner.]

Yes, please. _____

2. Which do you think is better, a credit card or cash?
[think a — card — .] [safer — convenient.]

_____

3. Are you going to buy this backpack?   [No, — not — enough.] [too small.]

_____

71

Listening 2: Conversation

A *Read this information about shirt sizes and fill in the blanks in the conversations below.*

シャツのサイズについての情報を読んで、下の会話の空所を埋めましょう。

Japanese Sizes vs. American Sizes

Japanese men's shirt sizes	Centimeters		Inches		American men's shirt sizes
	Collar	Chest	Collar	Chest	
S	33-34	81-87	12-13.5	32-34	XS
M	35-37	88-94	14-14.5	35-37	S
L	38-39	96-102	15-15.5	38-40	M
XL	40-42	104-110	16-16.5	41-43	L

1. A: I'm looking for a shirt. I'm a medium in Japan.

   B: Well, if you're a medium in Japan, you should buy a _____ in the U.S.

2. A: What's your collar size?

   B: It's about 35 centimeters.

   A: 35? Well, that's about _____ in the U.S.

B *Shota goes to a department store with his American friend Richard to buy a shirt. Listen to the conversations, and circle T (true) or F (false) for the following sentences.*

ショウタはアメリカ人の友人リチャードとシャツを買うためにデパートに来ています。会話を聞いて、次の文が正しければ T、誤っていれば F を丸で囲みましょう。

🎧 DL 61, 62   ◉ CD 61   ◉ CD 62

1. Shota usually buys shirts in large in Japan.   T   F
2. The first shirt Shota looks at is too small.   T   F
3. The store has some American shirts in small.   T   F
4. Shota pays in cash.   T   F

Your Turn to Talk

A *Make a conversation by choosing the correct sentences in this chart.*

表にある正しいほうの文を選んで、会話を完成させましょう。

⬇ DL 63   ◎ CD 63

(A) Shop Assistant

(B) Customer

Can I help you?

☐ Yes, it's on the 3rd floor.
☐ Yes, I'm looking for a polo shirt.

☐ Well, they're over there.
☐ Well, they're in the fitting room.

☐ Yes, I know. Thank you.
☐ Thank you. Oh, these shirts are too big. I need something smaller.

☐ What nationality are you?
☐ What size are you?

☐ In Japan, I wear a medium.
☐ Well, I'm a student.

☐ So what's your shoe size?
☐ So what's your chest size?

☐ About 88 centimeters, I think.
☐ About 26 centimeters, I think.

☐ Oh, you have big feet.
☐ 88 centimeters? Well, that's about 35 inches in the U.S., so you need a small.

☐ So I need a medium. Thank you.
☐ I see. Thank you.

B *Now practice the conversation with a partner until you can say it without looking at the chart.*

表を見なくても言えるようになるまで、パートナーと会話を練習しましょう。

Review

Key Phrases

Make sentences using the Key Phrases you learned in this unit.

このユニットで学んだ Key Phrases を使って文を作りましょう。

1. A: Can I help you? Are you looking for anything _____?
   B: Yes, please. I'm looking for a _____. I think I _____ a medium.

2. This sweater is too small. I need a _____ one.

3. I can't put these sneakers on. They're too _____. They're not _____ enough.

Word Power!

Study this list of important new words and phrases in this unit. You can complete the list by adding more words that you learned.

Unit 11 で登場した重要語句のリストです。空所には、その他に新しく学んだ語句を自由に書き入れ、オリジナルのリストを作りましょう！

English	Japanese
☐ bank account	銀行口座
☐ bills (U.S., Can.) = notes (U.K., Aus., N.Z.)	紙幣
☐ ATM	現金自動預け払い機
☐ in addition	さらに、その上に
☐ first few days	最初の数日
☐ anything special	何か特別なもの
☐ souvenir	お土産
☐ inch	インチ（長さの単位＝ 2.54cm）
☐ collar	襟
☐ chest	胸
☐ short-sleeved (shirt)	半袖の（シャツ）
☐ button-down (collar)	ボタンダウンの（襟）
☐ receipt	レシート、領収書
☐ fitting room	試着室
☐	
☐	
☐	
☐	
☐	
☐	
☐	
☐	
☐	

Unit 12

Safety on Campus

Unit Goals

● Talk about an incident　　　　　　トラブルについて話す
● Give details about an incident　　　当時の状況を伝える
● Describe lost property　　　　　　遺失物について説明する

Warm-up

Read the following notice. Who is it from?

お知らせを読みましょう。誰からのお知らせでしょうか。

⚠️ Your Safety on Campus ⚠️

● When you come to the campus, do not ¹(use an ATM / carry a lot of money).

● Keep your purse, wallet, or cell phone ²(out of sight / in sight).

● Don't leave your bag open. ³(Zip it up / Cover it up).

● Walk in well-lit places in the evening.

● In an emergency — fire, crime, or accident — phone Public Safety at 121.

Newton University Public Safety Office

Listening 1: Short Talk

A *Listen to the talk and choose the correct answers in the brackets above.*

話を聞いて、上のお知らせの 1 ～ 3 の（　　）内のうち正しいほうを選びましょう。

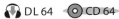 DL 64　 CD 64

B *Look at the script and listen again. Fill in the blanks.*

スクリプトを見ながら音声をもう一度聞いて、空所を埋めましょう。

🎧 DL 64   ◎ CD 64

Before we start class today, I'd like to tell you what happened **1.**_____. It seems that a wallet was stolen in the computer room. It belonged to a Thai student who was doing her homework there at lunchtime. Her Louis Vuitton wallet was in her bag. But she left the bag on a **2.**_____ and forgot to zip it up, so it was **3.**_____ for someone to see it. Also, she came here after getting some money from an ATM, so she had about **4.**_____ dollars in her wallet.

Now, we don't want this to happen again, so please don't carry a lot of cash on campus and don't forget to zip up your bag. You should always keep your valuables out of sight. Do you understand?

Check with Your Partner!

With a partner, ask and answer these questions about the script.

上のスクリプトについて、ペアになって1〜3の質問をお互いにしてみましょう。

1. Why was the student in the computer room?
2. What happened to her wallet?
3. What's her wallet like?

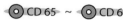

Key Phrases

What happened? - I lost … / I left it … / It was stolen …

🔊 What happened?

- I lost my cell phone. I left my bag in the cafeteria, and I think my phone was stolen from the bag.

I was …ing

🔊 I was shopping in the university drugstore. When I got to the checkout, I noticed my purse was missing.

What's … like? - It's … / It's made of …

🔊 What's your wallet like?

- It's a Louis Vuitton wallet. It's dark brown.
- It's about this big. (*gesture with hands*) It's made of leather.

Practice

Answer these questions using the words in the brackets.

[   ] 内の語句を使って、質問に答えましょう。

1. What happened?   [lost — umbrella.] [left — a classroom.]

_____

2. What were you doing at that time?   [Actually, — sleeping — the library.]

_____

3. What's your bag like?   [a shoulder bag.] [dark green — leather.]

_____

Listening 2: Conversation

A *Look at this notice and answer the questions below.*

掲示を見て、下の質問に答えましょう。

Newton University Public Safety

James Wilson Building, 1st floor
We are open 24 hours a day, seven days a week.

Our service includes:

- · 24-hour safety escort service
- · Fire safety
- · Medical assistance

- · Regular patrol on campus
- · Lost & found
- · Safety education

Email: publicsafety@newtonu.edu
24-Hour Emergency Line: 121
24-Hour Non-Emergency Line: 234-567-8911

Which service do you need if:

1. you fall down and hurt your leg? _____

2. you need to walk across campus to your dormitory late at night?

_____

3. you lose your bag on campus? _____

B *Listen to the conversation between Mari and a Newton University Public Safety employee, and circle T (true) or F (false) for the following sentences.*

マリとニュートン大学の学内警備員の会話を聞いて、次の文が正しければ T、誤っていれば F を丸で囲みましょう。

 DL 68   CD 68

1. Mari's dictionary is black and it's in a dark blue case.　　　　**T F**

2. Someone handed in her dictionary early this morning.　　　　**T F**

3. She has to fill out a form to get her dictionary back.　　　　**T F**

78

Your Turn to Talk

A *Look at this police report and write appropriate questions for each item.*

警察の紛失届を見て、各項目（1～8）について尋ねる質問を完成させましょう。

Police – Lost Property Report

1. **Name:** Taro Yamanaka
2. **Address:** 38 Main Street, Walton   3. **Tel. no.:** 086-296-767
4. **Lost item:** Wallet
5. **Description:** Dark brown, leather   6. **Contents:** $80, Visa card
7. **Where lost:** Walton Mall   8. **When lost:** About 11 a.m.

   Signature: Taro Yamanaka   **Date:** 8/27/2020

---

1. What's your name?
2. What's your _____ ?   3. What _____ ?
4. What did _____ ?
5. What _____ ?   6. What _____ ?
7. Where did _____ ?   8. When _____ ?

B *Now work with a partner. Imagine one of you lost something and the other is a police officer. Ask and answer questions about the incident.*

ペアワークです。一人は何かを紛失した人、もう一人は警察官になり、その出来事について質疑応答をしましょう。

Review Key Phrases

Make sentences using the Key Phrases you learned in this unit.

このユニットで学んだ Key Phrases を使って文を作りましょう。

1. I lost _____ this morning. I think I left it _____ .
2. I was _____ when I fell down and broke _____ .
3. My cell phone is a/an _____ . It's _____ .

Word Power!

Study this list of important new words and phrases in this unit. You can complete the list by adding more words that you learned.

Unit 12 で登場した重要語句のリストです。空所には、その他に新しく学んだ語句を自由に書き入れ、オリジナルのリストを作りましょう！

English	Japanese
☐ safety	安全
☐ out of sight / in sight	見えないところに／視界に入って、見えて
☐ zip up	ジッパーを締める
☐ well-lit	照明で明るい
☐ emergency	緊急事態
☐ crime	犯罪
☐ public safety	大学内での安全を守るための部署
☐ leave it (there)	それを（そこに）置き忘れる
☐ valuables	貴重品
☐ cell phone	携帯電話
☐ (be) missing	なくなっている
☐ safety escort	防犯のための付き添い
☐ lost & found	遺失物取扱所
☐ medical assistance	応急手当
☐ late at night	夜遅く
☐ fill out a form	用紙に書き込む
☐ electronic dictionary	電子辞書
☐ (be) relieved	ほっとした
☐ lost item	紛失物、なくしもの
☐ description	描写、説明
☐ contents	中身
☐	
☐	
☐	

Talking about Your Hometown

Unit Goals

● Talk about your hometown   出身地について話す
● Explain what you can do there   そこで何ができるのか説明する
● Talk about places of interest   名所について話す

Warm-up

Look at these photos of places to see in Kobe and complete the names.

神戸の名所の写真を見て、それぞれの名称を完成させましょう。

Places to See in Kobe

a. Ij_____

Western-style residences built during the Meiji and Taisho periods

b. _____
Kaikyou Bridge

the longest suspension bridge in the world

c. Ch_____

a popular shopping and dining district in central Kobe

Listening 1: Short Talk

A *Listen to a student talking about his hometown and answer these questions.*

日本人学生が出身地について話しているのを聞いて、次の質問に答えましょう。

 DL 69   CD 69

1. How many foreign residents are there in Kobe?   _____ thousand
2. What is the population of Kobe?   _____ million
3. Which coffee company was founded in Kobe?   _____

B *Look at the script and listen again. Fill in the blanks.*

スクリプトを見ながら音声をもう一度聞いて、空所を埋めましょう。

🎧 DL 69　💿 CD 69

My hometown Kobe doesn't have a long history like Kyoto. However, I learned several interesting things about it in junior high school. When Japan was opened at the end of the **1.**_____ era, Kobe was one of the first **2.**_____ ports and many foreign people came to live there. During the Meiji and Taisho periods, many western-style residences called *Ijinkan* were built. Today there are 50,000 foreign residents in the city among a total population of about 1.5 million.

Kobe has many well-known companies, including ASICS, Kawasaki Heavy Industries, Kobe **3.**_____, and UCC Coffee. You can also try the famous Kobe beef, and there are many **4.**_____ companies such as Juchheim, Morozoff, and Goncharoff. Interestingly, Kobe was one of the first cities in Japan to have a co-op, and Coop Kobe is still very successful today.

Check with Your Partner!

With a partner, ask and answer these questions about the script.

上のスクリプトについて、ペアになって１〜３の質問をお互いにしてみましょう。

1. Why are there many foreign residents in Kobe?
2. There is a famous sports shoe maker in Kobe. What is it called?
3. Which well-known food can you try in Kobe?

Key Phrases

There's a ... / There are ...

🔊 There's an active volcano in Kagoshima called Sakurajima.
There are some very good hot springs on the Satsuma Peninsula.

You can ... (you = anybody)

🔊 What can you do in Nagoya?
- You can watch a baseball game at Nagoya Dome.
- You can try *miso katsu*, which is deep-fried pork cutlet with *miso* sauce.

It's called ... / It's named after ...

🔊 The symbol of Sapporo is a clock tower. In Japanese, it's called Tokeidai.
Shiroi Koibito Park is named after a famous cookie made by Ishiya.

Practice

Answer these questions using the words in the brackets.

[   ] 内の語句を使って、質問に答えましょう。

1. Is there a night view in Hakodate?   [It — one — the best — Japan.]
Yes, there is, from Mount Hakodate. _____

2. What can you eat in Hakodate?   [You — seafood.] [It — delicious — not expensive.]

_____

3. What can you see there?   [It — Goryoukaku.] [built — the Edo period.]
You can see a Western-style fort. _____

_____

Listening 2: Conversation

A *Fill in the blanks in this chart of famous places and events in Japan.*

日本各地の名所と行事についての表の空所を埋めましょう。

The 3 Best ... in Japan (?)

Gardens: Kairakuen / **1.** K   / Korakuen

Views: Matsushima / Miyajima / **2.** A

Hot Springs: **3.** A   / Kusatsu / Gero

Castles: Himeji / Matsumoto / **4.** K

Night Views: Hakodate / **5.** K   / Nagasaki

Festivals: **6.** G   / Tenjin / Kanda

Do you agree? Are these really the best?

B *Listen to the conversation between Koji and his Brazilian classmate Paulo, and circle T (true) or F (false) for the following sentences.*

コウジとブラジル人のクラスメイトのパウロの会話を聞いて、次の文が正しければ T、誤っていれば F を丸で囲みましょう。

🎧 DL 73   💿 CD 73

1. Koji's hometown is on the Pacific Ocean side of Japan.	T	F
2. The name of his hometown is Kanagawa.	T	F
3. There are many traditional houses in the city where he lives.	T	F
4. Another place to visit is Kenrokuen, a famous Japanese garden.	T	F
5. As for souvenirs, you can buy some Kutani pottery.	T	F

Your Turn to Talk

A *Fill in the blanks below with details about your hometown.*

あなたの出身地についての詳細を、下の空所に書き入れましょう。

My Hometown

1. City name: _____   **2.** Location: _____

3. Population: _____   **4.** What to see: _____

5. What to buy: _____

6. What to do: _____

7. Well-known companies: _____

8. Famous people: _____

9. Best thing about my city: _____

B *Now work with a partner, and ask and answer these questions.*

ペアワークで次の質問に答えましょう。

1. What's the name of your hometown?   **2.** Where is it?

3. What's the population?   **4.** If I visit, what can I see?

5. What can I buy?

6. What else can I do?

7. Are there any well-known companies in your city?

8. Were any famous people born in your city?

9. What's the best thing about your city?

Review Key Phrases

Make sentences using the Key Phrases you learned in this unit.

このユニットで学んだ Key Phrases を使って文を作りましょう。

1. In my hometown, there's a _____ . There are also _____ .

2. If you visit my grandfather's hometown, you can _____ .

3. Himeji Castle is _____ Shirasagijou because _____ .

Word Power!

Study this list of important new words and phrases in this unit. You can complete the list by adding more words that you learned.

Unit 13で登場した重要語句のリストです。空所には、その他に新しく学んだ語句を自由に書き入れ、オリジナルのリストを作りましょう！

English	Japanese
☐ residence	住宅、邸宅
☐ Meiji period (era)	明治時代
☐ suspension bridge	（大規模な）つり橋
☐ district	地区
☐ resident	住民
☐ found	創立する
☐ heavy industry	重工業
☐ steel	鋼鉄
☐ try	試す、試食する
☐ co-op	（生活）協同組合
☐ well-known	よく知られた、有名な
☐ volcano	火山
☐ hot spring	温泉
☐ peninsula	半島
☐ (be) called	～と呼ばれている
☐ (be) named after	～にちなんで命名された
☐ fort	砦
☐ rule	統治する
☐ pottery	陶磁器
☐	
☐	
☐	
☐	
☐	

Information

Unit Goals

- Understand notices and messages   掲示や連絡事項を理解する
- Explain the content of notices and messages   掲示や連絡事項の内容を説明する
- React to notices and messages   掲示や連絡事項に対応する

Warm-up

Read this notice on the ELC bulletin board. What kind of people are they looking for?

ELC の掲示板の連絡事項を読みましょう。どんな人たちを求めているのでしょうか。

こんにちは

Japanese Language Partners

きてね！

Can you speak Japanese? Please join our Japanese Conversation Lounge!

When: Every Wednesday from 4:00 p.m. to [1](6:00 p.m. / 6:30 p.m.)

Where: East Asian Studies [2](Room 21 / Common Room)

Free refreshments!

Please contact Jennifer Evans (jevans@newtonu.edu) or just come on Wednesday at 4 o'clock.

East Asian Studies Dept. — Japanese Speaking Society

Listening 1: Short Talk

A *Listen to the talk and choose the correct answers in the brackets above.*

話を聞いて、上の掲示物の 1 ～ 2 の（　　）内のうち正しいほうを選びましょう。

 DL 74   CD 74

B *Look at the script and listen again. Fill in the blanks.*

スクリプトを見ながら音声をもう一度聞いて、空所を埋めましょう。

DL 74　CD74

Japanese Language Partners

If you can speak Japanese and have some **1.**_____ time on Wednesday afternoons, would you like to help us?

Every Wednesday from 4:00 p.m. to 6:00 p.m. we hold a Japanese Conversation Lounge in the East Asian Studies Common Room, and we are looking for Japanese-speaking **2.**_____ to join us. We chat in Japanese for one hour over coffee and then switch to English for an hour. This is a great chance to share your culture and also **3.**_____ up your English-speaking ability. If you are **4.**_____, please contact Jennifer Evans in the East Asian Studies Department or just come to the Common Room next Wednesday at 4 o'clock.

East Asian Studies Dept. – Japanese Speaking Society (JSS)

Check with Your Partner!

With a partner, ask and answer these questions about the script.

上のスクリプトについて、ペアになって1〜3の質問をお互いにしてみましょう。

1. Who's the message from?
2. What's it about? (*Hint: Look at the title.*)
3. What do they do first at the Japanese Conversation Lounge?

DL 75 ~ 77   CD 75 ~ CD 77

Who's ... from? / What's ... about?

🔊 Who's the email from? - It's from the Student Services office.
What's it about? - It's about the university festival.

What does ... say? - It says (that) ...

🔊 What does the notice say?
- It says they are looking for volunteers.
- It also gives the time and place of the meeting.

It sounds ...

🔊 It sounds interesting. I think I'll check it out.
It sounds like fun, but I don't think I have time on Friday.

Practice

Answer these questions using the words in the brackets.

[   ] 内の語句を使って、質問に答えましょう。

1. What does the email say?   [a meeting — held — 7:00 p.m. — Friday.]

It says that _____

2. What's it about?   [They — going — talk — Studio Ghibli.]

It's about Japanese *anime*. _____

3. So, are you going to attend?   [Yes, — think — go.] [It — interesting.]

_____

Listening 2: Conversation

A *Practice reading this notice aloud with a partner. Then answer the questions below.*

次の掲示を読み上げる練習をパートナーとしましょう。その後、下の質問に答えましょう。

 Notice: Library Closure

The university library will be closed on Saturday, June 17th for repairs to the building's air conditioning system. Books that are due on Saturday can be returned on Monday. Students will still be able to use the library's computer system from outside the library. The library will open again at 8:30 a.m. on Monday, June 19th. We are very sorry for any inconvenience this may cause.

James Hudson, Head Librarian

1. Who's this notice from?

It's from _____.

2. What does it say?

It _____ the library will be _____ on June 17th.

B *Listen to the conversation between Shota and Janine about the notice, and circle T (true) or F (false) for the following sentences.*

上の掲示についてのショウタとジャニーンの会話を聞いて、次の文が正しければ T、誤っていれば F を丸で囲みましょう。

1. They are looking at a website.　　　　　　　　　　　　　　T　F

2. It says the library will be open tomorrow.　　　　　　　　T　F

3. Janine needs to borrow some books from the library.　　T　F

4. The report deadline is tomorrow.　　　　　　　　　　　T　F

5. They decide to go to the library immediately.　　　　　　T　F

Your Turn to Talk

A *Read this message on the ELC bulletin board and answer these questions.*

ELC の掲示板の連絡事項を読んで、下の質問に答えましょう。

End-of-Term Examinations

Class examinations for the winter term will be held as follows:

Intermediate Class		
	Thursday, February 27th	Friday, February 28th
9:00-10:00 (Room 23)	Reading and Listening	Movie English
10:40-11:40 (Room 17)	Grammar and Writing	Global Issues

Note: Students cannot use dictionaries.

Jackie Smith, Course Director

1. Who's it from? _____
2. What's it about? _____
3. What does it say about dictionaries? _____

B *Now work with a partner and talk about each test like this.*

ペアワークでパートナーとそれぞれのテストについて次のように話しましょう。　🎧 DL 80　💿 CD 80

A: When will the *Reading and Listening* test be held?

B: It'll be held on *Thursday, February 27th* from *9:00 to 10:00*.

A: Does it say where?

B: Yes, it says *Room 23*.

Review Key Phrases

Make sentences using the Key Phrases you learned in this unit.

このユニットで学んだ Key Phrases を使って文を作りましょう。

1. There's a _____ on the bulletin board _____ the class party.
2. It _____ the party will be _____ on Saturday, March 1st _____ 7:00 p.m. to 11:00 p.m. _____ the ELC Common Room.
3. The party _____ like fun. I think I'll go.

Unit 14
Word Power!

Study this list of important new words and phrases in this unit. You can complete the list by adding more words that you learned.

Unit 14 で登場した重要語句のリストです。空所には、その他に新しく学んだ語句を自由に書き入れ、オリジナルのリストを作りましょう！

English	Japanese
☐ notice	掲示、（告示用の）張り紙
☐ message	連絡事項、通知
☐ bulletin board (noticeboard)	掲示板
☐ East Asian Studies	東アジア研究
☐ common room	（学校等の）休憩室
☐ refreshments	軽い飲食物
☐ brush up	〜の技術（知識）に磨きをかける
☐ Student Services	学生課
☐ check ... out	調べる
☐ closure	閉鎖
☐ (be) due	返却期限の
☐ inconvenience	不便
☐ deadline	締め切り、最終期限
☐ Oh dear!	あら、まあ！
☐ end-of-term examination	学期末試験
☐ global issues	グローバルイシュー、地球規模の問題
☐	
☐	
☐	
☐	
☐	
☐	
☐	
☐	

15 Farewell

Unit Goals

- Say goodbye
- Thank people
- Talk about future hopes and plans

さよならを言う
感謝の気持ちを表す
将来の希望と計画を話す

Warm-up

Read this notice about a farewell dinner and answer the questions below.

送別会のお知らせを読んで、下の質問に答えましょう。

Newton University English Language Center
Farewell Dinner
for
Students in the Autumn Intensive Program

Time: Wednesday, December 15th, 7:00-9:30 p.m.
Location: Richmond Room, The Hub Student Center, City Campus

Farewell Speech: Jeremy Craven, Director, Newton University International
Exchange Center
Presentation of Certificates: Helen Winsford, Head of ELC
Speech by Student Representative: Makiko Ikeda

---

1. Who is the dinner for? _____
2. Where is it going to be held? _____
3. How many people will make a speech? _____

Listening 1: Short Talk

A *Listen to Makiko's speech and answer this question.*

マキコのスピーチを聞いて、次の質問に答えましょう。

🎧 DL 81　💿 CD 81

Who does Makiko thank?
She thanks the ELC _____, the ELC _____ and the _____.

B *Look at the script and listen again. Fill in the blanks.*

スクリプトを見ながら音声をもう一度聞いて、空所を埋めましょう。

🎧 DL 81 　 💿 CD 81

Ladies and gentlemen, good evening! First of all, I would like to say thank you to the teachers of the English Language Center. Your lessons were always interesting and we have learned the joy of ^{1.}_____ in English from you.

Secondly, let me say thank you to the ELC staff for your careful organization and for arranging so many wonderful ^{2.}_____ . We will always remember the sightseeing trips, the visits to local schools, and the great evening entertainment that you organized for us.

Finally, and most importantly, thank you to the host families. You have looked after us so well and made our stay really ^{3.}_____ .

Thank you, everybody, and good luck to you all. I ^{4.}_____ to see you again one day!

Check with Your Partner!

With a partner, ask and answer these questions about the script.

上のスクリプトについて、ペアになって１～３の質問をお互いにしてみましょう。

1. Does Makiko thank the teachers for their lessons?
2. Does she thank the teachers for arranging trips?
3. What does Makiko hope to do?

DL 82 ~ 84   CD 82 ~ CD 84

Key Phrases

Have a … / Don't forget to … / Take care! / Good luck!

A: Have a good flight!
B: Thanks.
A: And don't forget to send me an email.
B: Don't worry, I won't.
A: OK. Take care! Good luck!
B: Thanks, I will. Bye!

Say thank you to … / Thank you for …

Please say thank you to John for me.
Thank you for your help. Thank you for teaching me.

I'm planning to … / I'm thinking of …ing / I hope to …

I'm planning to study hospitality.
I'm thinking of working in the tourist industry.
I hope to work at a big international hotel.

Practice

Complete the responses.
応答を完成させましょう。

1. A: Have a good trip!   B: Th_____ _____.
　　A: And don't forget to call me!   B: Don't _____ . I _____.

2. A: Please say thank you _____ your mother _____ me.
　　B: Yes, I will.
　　A: And thank you _____ all your help.
　　B: Not at all.

3. What are you thinking of doing in the future? (*Use your imagination!*)

_____

95

Listening 2: Conversation

A *Read the list of things Makiko would like to do after she goes back to Japan, and fill in the blanks. Then, make three sentences about her.*

マキコが帰国後にしたいと思っていることのリストを読み、空所に入る単語を選んで書き入れましょう。その後、マキコについて文を３つ作りましょう。

PLANNING	· do an ¹( ) · keep in touch with the Bentons · get a driver's ²( )
THINKING	· ³( ) for a job in a travel agency · do some volunteer work · ⁴( ) around Japan
HOPE	· speak ⁵( ) every day · get a good job · visit the Bentons again

apply   travel   internship   license   English

· PLANNING: Makiko is _____ .
· THINKING: She's _____ .
· HOPE: She _____ .

B *Listen to the conversation between Katrina and Makiko and circle T (true) or F (false) for the following sentences.*

カトリーナとマキコとの会話を聞いて、次の文が正しければ T、誤っていれば F を丸で囲みましょう。

DL 85   CD 85

1. Makiko is planning to do an internship at a hotel.   **T   F**
2. Steve is probably going to drive Makiko to the airport.   **T   F**
3. Katrina and Makiko are going to miss each other.   **T   F**
4. They will keep in touch by letter.   **T   F**

Your Turn to Talk

A *Make a conversation by choosing the correct sentences in this chart.*

表にある正しいほうの文を選んで、会話を完成させましょう。

DL 86　　CD 86

(A) Student

Oh, it's time to go. It's already 10:30.

☐ I'm going to miss you too. I hope I can come again.
☐ Thanks. It was delicious.

☐ Yes, I had a nice time.
☐ Thanks!

☐ No, I don't think so.
☐ Don't worry, I won't.

☐ Yes, see you. Bye.
☐ Yes, I will. Thanks.

(B) Host mother

☐ Yes, it's time for lunch.
☐ Really? Oh, we're really going to miss you.

☐ Yes, I think so too. Have a nice time!
☐ I hope so too. Well, have a good trip!

☐ And don't forget to email me.
☐ And take care of yourself.

☐ OK. Well, see you again.
☐ OK. Well, don't get lost.

B *Now practice the conversation with a partner until you can say it without looking at the chart.*

表を見なくても言えるようになるまで、パートナーと会話を練習しましょう。

Review Key Phrases

Make sentences using the Key Phrases you learned in this unit.

このユニットで学んだ Key Phrases を使って文を作りましょう。

1. A: I hope you _____ a nice holiday in Singapore.　B: Thanks.
2. A: Thank you for looking _____ me.　B: Not at all.
3. A: Have a nice weekend!　B: Thanks, you _____.
4. A: Don't forget to call me next week.　B: Don't worry. I _____.
5. A: Please say thank you to Mrs. Smith.　B: OK. I _____.
6. I hope to _____ to university next year. I'm thinking of _____ the entrance exam in October. I'm planning to _____ in the library all summer.

Word Power!

Study this list of important new words and phrases in this unit. You can complete the list by adding more words that you learned.

Unit 15 で登場した重要語句のリストです。空所には、その他に新しく学んだ語句を自由に書き入れ、オリジナルのリストを作りましょう！

English	Japanese
☐ farewell	さよなら、別れ
☐ farewell dinner	送別会
☐ intensive program	集中コース
☐ certificate	修業証書
☐ representative	代表
☐ joy	喜び
☐ arrange	計画・手配する
☐ entertainment	娯楽
☐ memorable	忘れ難い
☐ Take care!	気をつけてね！
☐ Say thank you to ... (for me).	（私に代わって）〜にお礼を言ってください。
☐ hospitality	歓待、親切なもてなし
☐ keep in touch	連絡を取り合う
☐ apply for	〜に申し込む
☐ travel agency	旅行代理店
☐ miss (someone)	〜がいなくて寂しく思う
☐ Not at all.	いえいえ、とんでもない。
☐	
☐	
☐	
☐	
☐	
☐	
☐	

List of Useful Classroom Expressions

▶□ 遅れてすみません。
　　I'm sorry I'm late.

▶□ 寝坊しました。／事故で電車が遅れました。／バスに乗り遅れました。／具合が悪かったんです。
　　I overslept. / My train was delayed because of an accident. /
　　I missed the bus. / I was sick.

▶□ 〜はどういう意味ですか。
　　What does "..." mean?

▶□ 〜は英語で何と言いますか。
　　How do you say "..." in English?

▶□ 〜のスペル（綴り）を教えてください。
　　How do you spell "..."?

▶□ 今やっているのは何ページですか。
　　What page are we on?

▶□ 今は何をやる時間ですか。
　　What do we have to do now?

▶□ すみません、質問は何でしたか。
　　Sorry, what was the question?

▶□ わかりました。／わかりません。
　　OK, I understand. / I'm sorry, I don't understand.

▶□ もう少し大きな声で話してくれますか。
　　Could you speak a little louder, please?

▶□ もう一度説明してくれますか。
　　Could you explain that again?

▶□ もう一度繰り返してくれますか。
　　Could you repeat that, please?

▶□ 手伝っていただけますか。
　　Could you help me, please?

▶□ 今日の宿題は何ですか。
　　What is today's homework?

▶□ 宿題の提出期限はいつですか。
　　When is the homework due?

▶□ すみません。宿題を家に忘れて来ました。
　　I'm sorry, I left my homework at home.

▶□ 最終試験はいつですか。
　　When is the final exam?

▶□ 辞書を使ってもいいですか。
　　Can I use the dictionary?

▶□ トイレに行ってもいいですか。
　　Can I go to the toilet/restroom?

▶□ あなたの番です。／私の番です。
　　It's your turn. / It's my turn.

▶□ 準備できました。／まだ準備できていません。
　　I'm ready. / I'm not ready yet.

▶□ ～を持ってくるのを忘れました。借りることはできますか。
　　I forgot to bring .... Can I borrow one/yours?

▶□ 気分がよくないです。早退してもよいですか。
　　I'm not feeling well. May I leave early?

▶□ ～なので、次回の授業は欠席します。
　　I'll be absent from the next class because ....

本書にはCD（別売）があります

Ready for Takeoff!
English for Study Abroad

短期留学・語学研修で学ぶ英語コミュニケーション

2020年 1 月20日　初版第 1 刷発行
2023年 4 月10日　初版第 3 刷発行

著者　　Alan Jackson
　　　　内田　ひろ子

発行者　　福 岡 正 人

発行所　　株式会社　金 星 堂

（〒101-0051）　東京都千代田区神田神保町 3-21
Tel　（03）3263-3828（営業部）
　　　（03）3263-3997（編集部）
Fax　（03）3263-0716
http://www.kinsei-do.co.jp

編集担当　西田　碧　　　　　　　　Printed in Japan
印刷所・製本所／萩原印刷株式会社

ISBN978-4-7647-4105-8　　C1082